THE DETECTIVE
AND THE DOCTOR

THE DETECTIVE
AND THE DOCTOR

A Murder Casebook

D.J. Cole & P.R. Acland

ROBERT HALE · LONDON

ISBN 0 7090 5355 X

Robert Hale Limited
Clerkenwell House
Clerkenwell Green
London EC1R 0HT

2 4 6 8 10 9 7 5 3 1

Photoset in New Century Schoolbook by
Derek Doyle & Associates, Mold, Clwyd.
Printed Great Britain by
St Edmundsbury Press Ltd, Bury St Edmunds, Suffolk.
Bound by WBC Bookbinders, Bridgend, Mid-Glamorgan.

Contents

We dedicate this book to past and present officers of West Mercia Constabulary who have helped the authors in the investigation of these and other murder inquiries.

Foreword

by Sir Thomas Hetherington

David Cole became the head of West Mercia CID in 1980 at a time when I was the Director of Public Prosecutions. I soon learnt, from those of my colleagues who were responsible for the prosecution of cases of serious crime in that part of the country, how highly he was regarded as a most competent and intelligent detective. In 1982 I had my first opportunity to meet David, when he found himself, rather unexpectedly, in charge of a major investigation into what emerged as one of the most serious spy cases since the Second World War, the trial of Geoffrey Arthur Prime. Because of the nature of the evidence, I personally supervised the preparation of the case for the prosecution, and thus rapidly came to see for myself David Cole's meticulous efficiency, his dedication to the task in hand, and his sympathetic and delicate handling of a case of extreme international sensitivity.

West Mercia seemed to have its full quota of serious crime during the 1980s, and on more than one occasion following the spy trial I saw the fruits of David's scrupulous investigations, in which he always kept clearly in mind the need to produce evidence which was admissible and credible. He did not hesitate to seek forensic and legal advice when that seemed desirable, and was very conscious of the problems and requirements of the various disciplines involved in the administration of the criminal law. His many successes were based on his realistic approach to each individual problem and his shrewd understanding of the vagaries of the criminal mind. These are among the characteristics which made David such a successful and highly respected detective, and they are well illustrated in this account of the unravelling of the murder cases with which he and Dr Peter Acland were involved.

Above all, I found David Cole to be humane and thoroughly professional. It was a great honour to work with him as a trusted friend and colleague, and I welcome the fact that he has found time during his very busy retirement from the police to write this fascinating book.

Sir Thomas Hetherington KCB, CBE, TD, QC
Director of Public Prosecutions, 1977–1987

Foreword

by Professor Bernard Knight

Peter Acland was, until very recently, a unique phenomenon on the British forensic scene in that he was the only full-time forensic pathologist to work independently outside the university or Health Service structure. Although his example has recently been followed by others in London and the North-West, it was Peter Acland who for many years dealt with much of the coroners' and criminal cases in the Birmingham and West Midlands area.

Peter Acland has been involved in a considerable number of notorious and sometimes controversial cases, some of which are described in this book, especially those where he collaborated with Detective Chief Superintendent David Cole in the investigation.

Like another forensic pathologist (whom modesty prevents me from mentioning!), Peter came up 'through the ranks' having been in military service and also having been a medical laboratory technician before entering medical school. This additional experience of life assists in widening the understanding of human activity and misbehaviour which is all too evident in the work of a forensic pathologist. Although books of forensic anecdotes and case reminiscences are usually reserved for the more senile years of a pathologist's life-span, Peter Acland had accumulated enough interesting cases to fuel a book by early middle age. I am sure that it will be a very interesting contribution to those many members of the public with an insatiable appetite for tales of criminality and their forensic solution.

Professor Bernard Knight CBE
Professor of Forensic Pathology, University of Wales College
of Medicine, and Home Office pathologist

9

Introduction

Senior detectives responsible for investigating the most serious criminal acts are a cautious breed: David Cole was no exception. They are also among life's greatest cynics, and Cole lived by the maxim that if things begin badly they rarely improve. On a Saturday morning in March 1984 circumstances forced him to abandon his natural caution and events confirmed the truth of his cynicism.

The detective was off duty, but 'on call' and should have known better than to start painting a bedroom. Inevitably, the telephone rang; the familiar voice of a uniform branch colleague was unusually hesitant:

'... the body of an old lady in a wood about four hundred yards off the road. She's well known, used to own Percy Thrower's nursery ... a country woman and keen walker ... but we think she's about seventy-five ... she may have been taken ill.'

He did not sound convinced by his own prognosis.

'We haven't touched the body, but there are some suspicious features. She hasn't got any pants on and her skirt is lying a few feet away. I think it's one you should have a look at.'

After a few questions Cole replaced the receiver equally convinced it was something he should look at, together with a forensic pathologist. His list of telephone numbers was in the car and as he went to retrieve it the front door slammed behind him; the back door was already locked and his wife and children were out.

Minutes later, after clambering up a ladder and through a bedroom window, he suppressed his irritation and started ringing round the expert consultants who normally assisted him. They were either unobtainable or already engaged on professional duties.

In desperation he called the control room at Force

Headquarters. 'Has the computer got anyone listed that I haven't got in my diary?'

'Have you tried Dr Peter Acland?'

'Who?'

'Dr Peter Acland – the Home Office put him on the official list a few weeks ago.'

'What's he like?'

It was a spontaneous yet stupid question. The police constable sitting in the glass-panelled sanctuary, surrounded by telephones and wireless paraphernalia, would probably never see a dead body, let alone examine a murder scene. He could only pass on a number.

Peter Acland was at home and he too had difficulties. Peter was caring for his young son while his wife accompanied their elder boy to hospital for a minor operation.

'There must be someone else available; Norman Gower? Ken Scott?'

'I've tried them all – even "Prof." Knight from Cardiff. You're the only one around.'

'Oh well, OK. I suppose I could get a babysitter – I'll be along.'

Getting hold of a babysitter was the least of his problems. Jane, a secretary at the medical school, answered the call and agreed to look after the home front. She was well aware of his dilemma.

'The Prof. will be furious if he finds out.'

Her reminder, though unnecessary, was probably the stimulant required to give Acland a shove in the direction he had been contemplating for some time.

'That's no problem. This is the first case I've done for West Mercia. I can't let them down. Besides, there's probably nothing in it – it'll be a quick post mortem and no one will be any the wiser. The Prof. will never even hear anything about it ...'

Acland was wrong on all counts.

To qualify in medicine had been his only reason for coming to Birmingham but he had stayed on at the University as a lecturer in pathology, at the same time developing a long-held interest in forensic matters. A forensic pathologist needs a good background in the generalities of his subject and at first the department tolerated his increasing involvement with the police.

For some time Acland had worked on an *ad hoc* basis,

trailing around behind his eminent predecessor, Dr Ben Davis. He had met Cole a few times but did not expect to be remembered. Eventually accepted as a peripheral member of the select band of pathologists who assisted the Midland police forces, representinig West Midlands, West Mercia, Staffordshire and Warwickshire forces, he successfully assisted in a couple of dozen murder cases and performed well when confronted by the firepower of some of the most formidable barristers.

But the national forensic pathology service was seriously undermanned and without formal organization. In the mid-eighties the universities and hospitals which provided the service were being squeezed financially and in Acland's case matters came to a head with a showdown between his employers and the Home Office. The latter acknowledged his ability and sought to grant him official status as a 'Home Office pathologist' – a position worth more in title than money.

The University took up the offer as an opportunity to wring more funding from central government. Their argument was that they should not be expected to provide cash or resources for a teaching pathologist to run round for the police when the funding should be the Home Office's responsibility. The only benefit to the medical school was the intangible kudos of having an appointee on their payroll. They had tolerated that very situation for twenty years and now decided to put their foot down.

Unfortunately the boot landed on Acland. The professor was not a man to be crossed and had a reputation for getting his own way. Acland was told he must not take on any more criminal cases – an instruction that he received a week before Cole's call. He had almost made up his mind to go freelance and provide a full-time forensic pathology service for the Midlands police forces; the call probably tipped the scales for him.

The two experts had beaten quite different paths to reach the positions they held in the world of homicide investigation. David Cole was steeped in police work since leaving school and by 1984 had a decade of service as a chief superintendent under his belt and was a veteran of murder investigations. He was uncompromising in his pursuit of criminals, to the point where he was often assessed as blunt, dogmatic and at times arrogant. Those who jumped to such conclusions very often had little understanding of the nature of his job.

The person who commands a criminal investigation department has a complex and exacting responsibility. His primary function is to oversee a department consisting of about a tenth of the total force establishment. The everyday task is to combat an ever-increasing burden of mundane crime while making provision for the investigation of major offences. Fortunately very few areas suffer homicide regularly enough to justify a permanent 'murder squad', so those particular investigations are undertaken by ordinary detectives under the direction of a small number of specialists. It is by the results this select group achieves that the general public largely judges its police force. Whether because of morbid curiosity or genuine concern there is nothing more likely to excite public opinion than an emotive murder.

The investigation of serious crime is a complicated business. The senior detective not only exercises control over operational matters but he must now be well versed in the practical uses, if not the detailed workings, of computers. Computers have been hailed as the panacea of all ills after inadequacies were identified in traditional manual systems – inadequacies never more spectacularly demonstrated than during the Yorkshire Ripper enquiry. Unfortunately reality often belies expectation and those who place their faith in machinery choose to ignore a basic deficiency – the inability of a computer to think for itself. While modern technology enhances storage and assists vital analytical processes it does little to advance the actual detection process. Unless strictly controlled a computer churns out information which can swamp an inquiry. The modern senior detective must be able to sort the wheat from the chaff and exercise judgement; these skills have evolved as his greatest responsibility and are the ones by which he will succeed or fail. With limited resources and from endless lists of possible lines of inquiry or suspects, he must have the foresight to select those few which may further his aim. In the glare of publicity he walks an unenviable tightrope.

The only common feature in Cole and Acland's background was that they both originated from Service families. The characteristic of Acland's early life was movement. His father was in the Royal Air Force and when Peter was a youngster the family left Ipswich for Bristol. When his father retired and obtained employment with the Reader's Digest company in

London he spent his adolescent years on the Essex border. Acland Senior's premature death forced his mother to move yet again back to Ipswich – perhaps having a teenaged son near London in the early 1960s was the prime reason.

They returned to Ipswich. Peter was never the most studious of pupils and at 16 had only a few mediocre O levels, just enough to continue into the sixth form. He didn't work hard and, apart from the sciences, he wasn't particularly interested. Anyway he found Ipswich pretty dull and resolved to leave home and do something exciting. At the same time, he might still study a bit of extra science.

He joined the Royal Marines; the idea of extra study didn't materialize but he learned a good deal about himself and human nature, as only the Services can teach. After two years he had had enough; the lust for adventure had worked itself out of his system and an old knee injury, aggravated by boxing, proved a legitimate avenue for early release.

He didn't want to return to Ipswich, favouring Bristol, where he obtained work as a pathology technician at the old Royal Infirmary. It was a teaching hospital and Acland rubbed shoulders with many medical students. He had always been led to believe that it was incredibly difficult to be accepted as a medical student; one had to be very clever and hard-working. But Acland wasn't too impressed with the intellectual ability of some of the students he met – once a medical student asked him where a particular consultant could be found. He pointed through a hatch to where the doctor was sitting. The medical student then climbed through the hatch instead of taking the more orthodox route via an adjacent door. As for hard work, the Marines had taught him that anything was possible with effort; he found chemistry easy and had no trouble picking up an A level in his own time, together with a distinction in his Ordinary National Certificate.

His difficulty came when all the medical schools to which he applied turned him down. Then he approached Birmingham University which would offer a place if he got another A level. Three months in which to study Zoology from scratch was a formidable task. Acland needed to absorb enough of the subject to get at least a C grade from private study at the same time as holding down a full-time job and undertaking work-related education. It was the hardest he ever worked, before or since, but having set himself the goal, he was determined. He gave it a damn good and successful try.

As a qualified doctor Acland developed his anatomical expertise and analysed his future. He watched and followed; he heard lectures by many of the leading forensic pathologists of the day – famous names from the past, such as Simpson and Camps, as well as present-day practitioners of equal ability. After five years he felt he had followed them around for too long but, like many things in life, he had to be in the right place at the right time to get a foot on the ladder.

The young pathologist had observed that, most of the time, his Home Office colleagues were called upon to visit a scene, perform an autopsy, reach a conclusion and then disappear until called to court to give evidence if a case ever ensued. He thought he could be more useful than that. He considered it important to develop a relationship with whoever he worked with on cases, so that he could be consulted at any time with problems, however small or seemingly irrelevant.

His plans had almost reached fruition when Cole called for his assistance.

It was unfortunate that they began their working relationship on a case which was to be bedevilled by many oblique distractions. Their efforts were often going to be obscured by publicity created by diversions which made unreasonable demands on their self-restraint.

Acland arrived at Hunkington, a hamlet nestling beneath Haughmond Hill to the north of Shrewsbury, at quarter to five. Cole had already been there for two hours – not kicking his heels, but organizing a major inquiry. He was already convinced he was dealing with murder. They were embarking on one of the most controversial investigations in recent times. Soon not only Acland's professor, but the world and his wife would know about their work.

The young pathologist was anxious to provide a service and develop good relationships with the senior detectives he worked with. He never developed a greater empathy than the one he enjoyed with Cole: they fed off each other's knowledge and experience as equals, and shared the same dry sense of humour and the maverick qualities of free spirits.

It was as well they hit it off straight away because there would be many days ahead to test any relationship. 1984 saw the beginning of an association which, over the next six years, would involve them in an unusual number of complex cases of horrific murder.

* * *

The light was beginning to fail by the time Acland reached the small wood; arc lights can only provide limited illumination and he worked quickly to get an overall picture of the scene before dark. That was precisely what Cole wanted him to do. There seemed to be a tense atmosphere among the police officers as the chief superintendent, with characteristic bluntness, told him he would appreciate an opinion pretty damn quick as to how the old lady had died. And, more particularly, when. The pathologist appreciated the reason for concern while he assessed the scene in front of him.

1   Rural Murder

The Hilda Murrell Case

Cole drove towards Shrewsbury ruefully reflecting upon another spoilt weekend. It was approaching lunchtime and he did not anticipate seeing his home again that day.

A police car met him on the outskirts of town and guided him through the maze of country lanes around Haughmond Hill to the flat fields beyond. They approached a group of policemen and passed a small white Renault embedded in the offside hedge; skids marked its passage across the road from the grass verge on the opposite side. Detective Chief Inspector Chris Furber emerged from the gaggle of policemen standing nearby. The vehicle belonged to the old lady and he pointed across a field towards a poplar coppice.

It was bitterly cold on the exposed plain and the waterlogged ground was evidence of two days' continuous rain.

Hilda Murrell's body lay twenty yards inside the wood, arms and legs splayed in death's grotesque contortions. She was only partially clothed and her pathetic limbs were exposed to the elements. A suspender belt, skirt and woollen sock lay a few yards away.

Cole leaned over the body. The right side of her face was badly bruised and there were several clean-edged cuts on the hands.

'There's no doubt about this – she's been murdered. Those cuts are defence wounds caused by trying to fend off a knife. When we get the clothing off we'll find some more stab wounds. She isn't wearing knickers – have we found any? She might have been sexually assaulted.'

Furber pointed out a pair of felt bootees lying adjacent to the hedgerow about thirty yards away.

19

'No knickers, but those bootees on the edge of the field might indicate she crawled some distance into the wood. We haven't searched the whole field yet so we don't know what more we'll find!'

There were a number of queries beginning to rumble around Cole's brain.

'Has it rained here today, Chris? The clothes are soaking wet but she doesn't seem particularly stiff. How long do you reckon she's been here?'

It hadn't rained since Friday and Cole had misread the condition of the body. It was becoming limp because rigor mortis was wearing off – he had thought it was just beginning. It was a good example of the necessity for a medical expert's presence.

There was an embarrassed silence. Chris Furber had been told about the old lady just before lunchtime and knew the circumstances of her disappearance would be unlikely to please the man with the job of finding her killer.

'We think she's probably been here since Wednesday lunchtime.'

'Hasn't anyone missed her? What about that car in the ditch – didn't anybody see that?'

Furber drew him away from other inquisitive listeners.

'If you'd care to walk across and have a look at the car while we wait for the pathologist I'll put you in the picture.'

Furber is a first-class detective. Steady and reliable, he is also a psychology graduate. He never needed his specialism more than during the walk across that field. The pair had worked closely for many years and he knew Cole could be as explosive as a tinderbox. Several times in as many minutes he thought he came close to lighting the fuse.

During his lunchbreak on the previous Wednesday a farm worker had cycled across the end of Hunkington Lane to meet his wife off the country bus. When they walked back about fifteen minutes later there was a small white car against the hedge a few hundred yards away. It had not been there those few minutes earlier, but it was commonplace for ramblers to park anywhere before setting off into the countryside.

The local farmer got a different impression when he passed by on his way to lunch. He could see that the vehicle was embedded in the hedge and thought someone might be injured, but there was no one near the car, and he forgot about it until he went past again later in the afternoon.

The local bobby was about to start a tour of his patch when he received the farmer's call. He was taking over the panda car his mate had been using during the day and was going to slip him home. He promised they would have a look on the way.

A quick check with his Control told the policeman the car belonged to Hilda Murrell of 52 Sutton Road, Shrewsbury, which was five miles away on the same side of town. Unfortunately, the computer couldn't tell him that she was seventy-eight years old. There were no keys in the ignition nor any sign of damage or blood. A thick book stuck firmly beneath the front wheel told him that someone had tried to extricate the car from the ditch. It was an unlikely act for a frail old lady, but he could not know that.

Although the young policeman knew the car had been in the ditch since early afternoon he made no attempt to contact the owner's home. He would have been unsuccessful; she was lying a few hundred yards away, gravely injured, but probably still alive. After a quick check of the hedgerows, he went about his business.

It must be presumed that the policeman forgot the car, because two days later it was still there. The farmer rang the main police station at Shrewsbury, but the operator passed the information back to the same local bobby. This time he did go to the owner's house in Sutton Road. It was dark and pouring with rain. He noticed a light shining through chinks in the curtains of a downstairs room and found a side door wide open; as he knocked he saw that rain had driven through into the hallway. Failing to get a response he ventured towards the lighted room. An open handbag lay on a table, amid an assortment of papers. After a few more shouts, he decided the house was unoccupied and asked his Control to ring the house every half hour until they received a reply. For some inexplicable reason he went no further into other rooms.

There was a far less blasé reaction the following day when the early-morning duty inspector examined the outstanding work sheet. He sent a constable straight to the house. They knew nothing more than the message asking for Hilda Murrell to be contacted about her abandoned car. The officer arrived about seven o'clock and found the unlocked door. He couldn't make anyone hear, so made enquiries in the neighbourhood and traced a nearby relative. She was unable to offer any suggestion about Hilda Murrell's whereabouts, so he checked local hospitals to make sure she hadn't been admitted as a result of the car crash. Then he returned to the house and checked every room. Inside the front door he found daily newspapers from the previous Wednesday and began to smell a rat. On the stairway, in a bedroom and the bathroom he saw signs of a disturbance.

Quickly leaving the house he contacted the inspector and a sense of urgency began to prevail.

The first policeman sent to Hunkington Lane that morning was a good old-fashioned country bobby, used to working on his own initiative. He quickly recruited the help of a gamekeeper's wife and her two dogs. Within minutes the trained gundogs scented something in the coppice and led the couple to Miss Murrell's body. From the time he had been called from his police station six miles away it had taken the trusty officer only fifty minutes to make his grim discovery.

Acland bent over the body for some minutes, taking in all he could see without causing unnecessary disturbance. Finally he straightened; he knew he would not be flavour of the month when he announced that he could not definitely say they were dealing in murder. He could see from her red and raw knees she had crawled some distance. That probably explained why the lower clothing had come adrift. The redness of those injuries also gave him the first suspicion that hypothermia might be related to the death. He did not discount the cuts to the palms of the hands and incisions on the face. Even when he found stab wounds through her coat towards the right side of her abdomen, he still wouldn't categorically confirm an unlawful killing.

The look on Cole's face as he explained his reluctance to commit himself would have reduced lesser mortals to quivering heaps, but Acland stuck to his guns.

Although he was relatively new to the job he'd seen others, apparently more experienced, rush to conclusions which they later had to change. Acland insisted on keeping his options open until he had as much information as possible. It was likely to be garbled and inaccurate in the initial stages and his caution was therefore justified. He was told that she was an eccentric, and loved bird-watching and nature. He had to find out whether she had a psychiatric history: could she have stabbed herself and crawled away to die? There might also be some recent medical condition which had led to mental confusion, or suicidal tendencies, in such an elderly person.

All these matters he explored with the husband of Miss Murrell's second cousin when he came to the mortuary to identify the body. He knew of no such problem; quite the opposite. Hilda Murrell was a bright, sprightly and cheerful elderly woman with a clear, intelligent mind. She was active and independent, despite arthritis and failing sight aggravated by blindness in one eye.

Although the deceased was a small, relatively frail woman of eight stones, the doctor already appreciated the difficulty of carrying such a weight across a ploughed field. The undertakers who came to remove the body from the wood were a father and son team. Their van could not get nearer than the road some four hundred yards away and they experienced difficulty negotiating the undergrowth and ditch which led out of the copse. It soon became evident that the older man would not be able to manage carrying the stretcher across the field. Much to the amusement of police officers standing near the road, Acland took over and, although he considered himself still comparatively fit, the shared weight began to tell as they staggered across the field. Later, when theories emerged and speculation increased about how and when the corpse found its way into the wood, he remembered the difficulties of that walk. Kidnap, torture and placement of the body in the copse two days after she had been abducted were some of the theories presented as the bandwagon gathered momentum.

The examination of the unclothed body of Hilda Murrell confirmed with certainty that she had been attacked. A stab wound penetrated right through the biceps muscle of the right arm. He couldn't envisage this being self-inflicted and, together with the cuts across the hands, it suggested the wounds had been caused by defensive movements. That was not the cause, however, of the five wounds on the stomach; nor were they likely to have been self-inflicted.

He had seen the evidence of erratic driving and the impact when the car swerved across the lane and became embedded in the hedgerow. Some of the bruises and injuries to the side of the face, the broken collarbone, and more bruising on the arms may have been due to the collision. Some of them may have been caused by the victim's falling or staggering about. But they were just as likely to have been caused by punches, rough handling or kicks.

There was one injury, however, which had certainly been deliberate: the crushing of the small bones and structures of the neck, most likely caused by an arm pushed against the front of the throat.

Cole wanted answers to three questions: How did she die? The stab wounds to the abdomen were not more than an inch or two deep. A couple had penetrated the liver immediately below the skin, but had caused little bleeding – perhaps half a cupful within the abdominal cavity. She had not died of blood loss. What Acland found was numerous shallow erosions of the stomach wall which, together with the bright red bruising to the knees, indicated death from hypothermia.

When did she die? It was very difficult to say. The body temperature was the same as the surrounding environment. At the scene rigor mortis was easily 'broken' and wore off quickly in the warmth of the mortuary. In the cold, wet weather of recent days it would not have taken an elderly woman many hours to succumb to her injuries. It is most probable she died on the Wednesday, a few hours after her car had been seen in the ditch at lunchtime.

Had she been sexually assaulted? There was no obvious injury or other indication. A little reddening next to a benign wart in that area could be naturally explained. Interference that hadn't left any physical evidence could not be ruled out, but Acland could not say that she had been indecently interfered with from his immediate examination.

The pathologist was pressed further. 'Given the car was seen at lunchtime – would she still have been alive when the copper arrived at about six o'clock?'

'Impossible to say. I'll only go as far as to say she would certainly have been dead by midnight.'

'Thanks a lot – that's all I bloody well need.'

Acland's diagnosis meant that the old lady had endured a lingering death and Cole was decidedly uneasy as he left the post mortem room to go to her house. He knew it was bound to be suggested that greater efforts might have discovered her while she was still alive. Acland had told him that the injuries had not been life-threatening in spite of her age.

If she had been found the detective would probably be listening to her now, propped up in a hospital bed, while she told him what had happened. Instead, she lay on a mortuary slab and he would have to try and piece the story together. He was a good three days behind the ball game and a lot of evidence had been washed away by rain. He was not amused.

It was likely to be a difficult inquiry and he needed all the help he could obtain from the media to persuade witnesses to come forward. He could well do without the more emotive aspects of Hilda Murrell's death distracting attention from his main purpose.

Walking slowly through the house he failed to understand why it had taken so long to appreciate something was amiss. Perhaps it was all down to experience; he had been to hundreds of burglaries over the years. But it all seemed patently obvious: the contents of an opened handbag spread across the table; telephone wires ripped from a junction box; drawers and cupboards lying open; a broken baluster lying on the stairway; framed prints strewn around a bedroom, along with a pair of knickers, knotted sheet and soiled handkerchief.

He was paid to think on his feet and make deductions. What had happened in this house? Why had Hilda Murrell been found five miles away? The initial attack on the old lady had certainly occurred in the house; for some reason she had been disposed of in open countryside.

The old lady was not wearing knickers yet Acland was sure any sexual assault had not amounted to full intercourse. Was there something significant about the pair lying on the bedroom floor? Did the knotted sheet and the broken baluster mean she had been tied to the stairway while her assailant searched the house? Had he taken anything? She lived alone in reclusive style and no one really knew what was there to be stolen.

It was past midnight when Cole walked into the police garage where the car was being examined. It was parked in the middle of a bank of powerful lights as scientists and photographers swarmed around.

'We found the ignition key in her coat pocket when we got to the mortuary, Herbie. Have you found any more keys in the car?'

Detective Sergeant Perriton was Cole's trusted and experienced scientific officer. They shared much the same character and often clashed verbally as they bounced ideas off each other. These duels were regularly mistaken for blazing rows by those who did not know them. The same people were usually astonished when their querulous relationship invariably came up with the right answers.

'There's a lot more to this than meets the eye, Gaffer.' Herbie had not yet examined the house, but had closely examined the car. 'No more keys, but the book under the front wheel – obviously came from the car. Whoever tried to drive it out knew it was front-wheel drive. The driver's door was jammed against the hedge. I can't see the old lady being able to clamber out of that side in her condition.'

More questions started to bubble through the brain. Hilda Murrell had the keys in her pocket, so when had the attempt been made to get the car out of the ditch. There was no blood in the car; when had she been attacked with the knife?

There were a great many imponderables going through their minds, but as yet they only knew part of the story. Herbie had found a Hamlet cigar wrapper in the car. A grapefruit lying on the back seat looked as if it had been run through with a knife. The fascia board in front of the passenger seat had been slashed several times. Had Hilda Murrell driven her car to Hunkington under threat of a knife? After the crash had she tried to escape across the field as her attacker tried frantically to get the car out of the ditch? That theory appeared to be torpedoed by the key in her pocket.

Cole knew more than his colleague; he had been at the post mortem and to the house. It was time they pooled information, and they sat long into the night discussing the possible sequence of events leading to Hilda Murrell's death.

Since early afternoon a group of detectives had been busy trying to piece together the victim's last hours and when Cole emerged from a couple of hours' sleep on Sunday morning they knew a lot more about her. An impatient press was waiting for news and demanded instantaneous answers. They had no time to wait for painstaking detective work. Speculation quickly gathered momentum as news of Hilda Murrell's death hit the news-stands and airwaves. Cole saw storm-clouds gathering. He knew questions were going to be asked about the failure to find the old lady alive. He had not been involved until three days after her death so it was not really his problem. But he was aware of the possible effect on his inquiry, and ventured to offer advice. He also knew he would be out front facing the press and cameras and would have to take the flak. A statement promising a full inquiry into the circumstances surrounding the discovery of the car and body would take the heat out of the situation. He was overruled. Unconvincing explanations were offered which only served to fuel further speculation and thereby threatened to frustrate the efforts of those dedicated to the task of finding the killer.

Hilda Murrell was a cultured, refined soul who succeeded as a businesswoman through a combination of assertiveness and commercial intuition. She joined her father in the family business after obtaining a degree at Cambridge and eventually became an international authority on traditional and miniature roses. In private life she was shy and retiring; very few people knew much about her apart from a small group of close friends. No one spoke of a man in her life and she was always self-conscious about a disfigured sightless eye, which she hid behind the brim of a floppy hat. In town she was more readily recognized for her hats than for any other reason.

When she sold her business to the television gardener, Percy Thrower, in the late 1970s, she continued her lifelong affair with nature and the environment. Her magnificent garden was a perpetual interest and she further indulged her quest for solitude at a holiday chalet in remote countryside on the Welsh border. Retirement brought other interests and concerns, though always connected with environmental issues. Although she had for many years participated in committee work she now actively and uncharacteristically involved herself in campaigns. Perhaps she thought that the sands of time were running out and she needed to do something positive before it was too late.

The nuclear industry became the main target and she concerned herself particularly with the disposal of waste material. She was not a person to indulge in half-measures and once committed to a cause gave it everything. Lengthy research led to unacceptable conclusions, and in the last months of her life she wrote a formal paper for presentation to the commission of inquiry concerning itself with the feasibility of building the Sizewell B power station in East Anglia.

It was her innocent and dedicated commitment to this cause which created much of the speculation about her death. Immediately after it occurred, a number of similarly committed people told investigators that she had expressed fears for her safety. Allegedly this was because her objections to the nuclear industry flew in the face of officialdom. As the stories proliferated it surprised Cole that none was ever substantiated by documentation or independent corroboration.

Hilda's closest relatives were a niece and nephew living in southern England. They kept in touch by letter and telephone, but visits were infrequent. Her only regular visitor was a young second cousin, who often called when she was in town. She visited the day before Hilda's death and they chatted happily about a lunch the elderly lady had arranged with an old friend the following day. It was remarkable to the sensible younger woman that Hilda Murrell always appeared free of personal worries and never made mention of the fears later referred to by casual acquaintances.

Hilda Murrell did not keep the lunch appointment. At the time she should have arrived she was being driven from her home towards death.

Hilda Murrell had left little time to change and travel the twenty miles to her friend's when she returned from a shopping trip at about noon on Wednesday, 21 March 1984. She had been to the bank and a supermarket before calling for a chat with a neighbour. There had been time to place some of her shopping in the pantry before she was disturbed. Whether an intruder walked through the unlocked door, or she heard a noise elsewhere in the house and went to investigate, is only guesswork.

About three quarters of an hour later her little car emerged from the gateway at speed. The old lady was slumped in the passenger seat and a bulky man sat hunched behind the steering wheel as the vehicle roared through the streets of Shrewsbury. He drove past the main police station and into the country, occasionally glancing anxiously at the forlorn figure beside him. His erratic driving was exaggerated because he had had no time to readjust the driver's seat to a more comfortable position. It was shortly before one o'clock when they were last seen. A young mother hurrying home to prepare her husband's lunch overtook the little Renault as it lurched along the road half a mile from Hunkington Lane. Hilda's driving licence and AA membership card were later found in the field alongside the lane. In a corner of another field leading to the coppice, searchers discovered her broken spectacles, wide-brimmed hat and a small kitchen knife.

In the early afternoon a middle-aged couple taking a stroll along the top of Haughmond Hill were startled by a heavily built man running past. They were accustomed to joggers

using the lanes, but there was something unusual about this
one. He looked distinctly out of condition and although he wore
training shoes he was dressed in a conventional grey jacket
and trousers. The runner headed for town, retracing the route
taken by Hilda Murrell's car.

Eventually sixty-nine people came forward who had seen the
car on its outward journey, or the unfit man running back
towards Shrewsbury. He was last seen, exhausted and
limping, near allotments adjacent to the northern by-pass.
Days of national publicity, following a police reconstruction,
brought hundreds of suggestions as to his identity.

A wise murder investigator neither jumps to conclusions nor
accepts anything at face value. It would however not be
overstating the case to suggest that David Cole confidently
placed some importance on a connection between the mystery
runner and the death of Hilda Murrell.

The behaviour of the killer was bizarre, but not unique. In
the weeks following the murder Cole and Acland scratched
their heads to establish a likely sequence of events which
would give them an insight into his mind. The attack on the old
lady appeared to have been carried out by an ineffectual, but
unpredictably violent individual. He had seemingly not
sexually assaulted his victim, but scientists later found traces
of human semen on her underslip and a handkerchief. She
must therefore have been subjected to some form of passive
activity intended to humiliate or intimidate. Her injuries had
undoubtedly been aggravated by age and infirmity, but the
stab wounds were badly directed and comparatively feeble in
execution.

The unsophisticated hallmarks of an opportunist thief
littered the house: lager taken from the drinks cabinet, and the
empty can disposed of in the first floor toilet; no search in
places a burglar would expect to find valuables; the rejection of
identifiable credit cards in favour of the ready cash she had
withdrawn from the bank that morning. All these characteristics indicated to the two investigators that her death was the
work of an inadequate rather than a skilled professional.

The killer gave little thought to the dangers of recognition
when he drove his victim through the busy streets. Hilda
Murrell had no doubt proved more than a handful. Everyone
said she would react spiritedly if a burglar invaded her
privacy.

His efforts to secure her to the stairway had failed, as

presumably had any attempt at sexual domination. (We do not know for certain, but the perceived circumstances of bondage and ejaculation and the absence of evidence of a recognized sexual assault create the possibility – it is not an uncommon feature in such cases.) He had to give himself time to get away because the alarm would be quickly raised on the heavily populated estate if he left her behind. He did not intend to kill the old lady and headed for open countryside where he could dump her. When he ran out of road on a sharp bend and unsuccessfully tried to drive the car from the ditch he was back to square one. He faced the same dilemma: how could he get away from this determined woman? He had planned to shove her out in the middle of nowhere, and abandon the vehicle miles away. Now he was forced to subdue her, and an assault initially intended to cause delay developed into a viciousness which led to tragedy.

Cole and Acland reached the conclusion that Hilda Murrell's death was the work of a bungler and their view was supported by profiling experts of the American FBI, to whom they submitted the evidence.

Unfortunately, the opinion of experts did not conform to the views of those who placed more sinister connotations on the matter. The media, already stimulated by the failure to discover Hilda Murrell's body, sensed a good story and speculation threatened to overshadow the investigation. Cole and his team of eighty detectives kept their heads down, concentrating on the task in hand. He left others to answer the questions; he had not created the problem and was determined he would have no part in it. But the jinx which beset the inquiry from the start re-emerged. A group of detectives working on the case let the side down and played right into the hands of the critics.

In any substantial team of individuals there are always irresponsible elements. Cole knew the risks of human frailty and at the beginning of every major inquiry routinely warned against complacency. The years had taught him some hard lessons; indiscretions often brought disastrous results.

His entreaties at the beginning of the Murrell inquiry had little effect on a small number of detectives seconded to him by the Regional Crime Squad. Sent to carry out specific enquiries in East Anglia, they saw fit to ignore instructions and instead toured local golf courses. Their neglect was discovered some time later when it was necessary to reinterview a witness to whom they had purportedly spoken: she said she had never been visited.

After three months' hard slog, Cole dreaded the consequences. He would now have to deploy precious resources to check all the work that had been allocated to the errant officers throughout the entire investigation. When news of their suspension from duty reached the press it was impossible to stem another tide of suspicion – and newsmen were not the only ones to see the potential for embarrassing the authorities further. Politicians and pressure groups were quick to appreciate the opportunity, and the effect was staggering. For weeks the issue of Hilda Murrell's death received the attention of national and international media. The damage caused to the investigation was devastating. More time was spent supplying answers to media queries than pursuing the killer. The opportunity to stem speculation had been missed at an early stage, and the resignation of two detectives and the disciplining of others did nothing to ease the situation. Things only worsened.

In November an article published in the *New Statesman* explored the theory that Hilda Murrell's house had been broken into by someone interested in her paper on nuclear waste. It also questioned whether the intruder acted in the belief that his victim had received sensitive information from her nephew, Robert Green, who for some time before the article had been expressing unease at the circumstances of his aunt's death. He had been employed as an intelligence officer in the Royal Navy at the time of the Falklands War.

Emphasis was given to the involvement of Special Branch detectives in the hunt, fuelling the popular misconception of conspiracy theorists that such officers are a race apart from normal policemen. Contrary to the assumption that they are controlled by the state for the benefit of Government, they in fact come under the direct control of the chief constable and are recruited from within the ranks of his own force. Their operational duties are managed by the officer in charge of the Criminal Investigation Department, and when Cole became short of detectives he employed his Special Branch team to work on those matters best suited to their aptitude and training. He stopped trying to explain this simple truth to those it didn't suit; it was a waste of breath.

The article was the precursor to a whole new can of worms. As the press had another field day, a prominent politician entered the fray.

In an adjournment debate in the House of Commons the Labour MP Tam Dalyell, long interested in the circumstances of the sinking of the Argentinian battleship *Belgrano* during the Falklands War, made a connection between his *cause célèbre* and the Murrell investigation. Dalyell claimed to have information that the old lady had been killed while Intelligence Officers searched her house for secret documents believed to have been deposited with her by her nephew, and which related to the sinking of the *Belgrano*. Robert Green, who had since retired from the Navy, was horrified by the suggestion that he had betrayed the trust of his former employers. But there is no more assiduous campaigner than Dalyell when he adopts a cause. He kept the matter alive for weeks with a series of parliamentary questions and press releases.

He refused to disclose the source of his information during a lengthy interview with Cole at the House of Commons. The MP was assertive, considerate and urbane, but unable to substantiate his allegations. Later, when the politician declared the detective a serious, relevant interrogator, he ended the statement with a considerable sting in the tail: 'I do find it a little strange that Detective Chief Superintendent Cole and his senior colleagues should dismiss me out of hand as they themselves were responsible for investigating the case of Geoffrey Prime ... He [Cole] must know a great deal about security.'

The implication may have been unintentional but it was quickly seized upon by those with vested interests in keeping the story alive: Cole was involved in a cover-up.

In 1982, David Cole gained an international reputation when, in a combination of skill and good fortune, he sent the KGB spy Geoffrey Prime to prison for thirty-eight years.

Prime's downfall was due to his unusual sexual pre-dilections. For years he obsessively telephoned young girls, making suggestive and sometimes obscene remarks. Eventually, this comparatively passive activity didn't satisfy him and he needed physical contact. His first attack was carried out near Cheltenham and exactly twelve months later he struck again, at Malvern. His method was always the same. Carrying a clip-board and pen he called at a house where he knew a young girl would be alone. On the pretence of giving her father a pre-arranged estimate for redecorating a room he would gain entry and viciously assault the child at knifepoint.

It was his misfortune that he chose to carry out the third attack in rural Herefordshire. Cole was alerted to the offence shortly after it occurred and quickly linked it to the previous incidents. The girl involved had endured a horrifying experience and the detective knew that, if undetected, the offender might go on to commit more serious assaults during which a child might lose her life.

The intensive inquiry he organized soon bore fruit and Prime's luck ran out. A group of field-workers saw his maroon Ford car speeding along a lane near the house; one of them remembered that the registration plate bore the suffix 'S'.

Cole had a print-out of identical vehicles prepared. The police national computer listed 426 people in the counties of Gloucestershire, Herefordshire and Worcestershire who owned maroon Ford Cortinas with the 'S' prefix. Detectives began visiting each one. Within seven days they had eliminated all those in Herefordshire and Worcestershire and moved into Gloucestershire. The first call they made was at Prime's home in Cheltenham. Although he denied responsibility he had made a fatal mistake when he carried out the crime. Scientists found his fingerprints inside the victim's house.

Some strange letters were found beneath his bed and a detailed search revealed the impedimenta of a spy. Prime, who had for some time been employed as an interpreter at the secret Government Communication establishment in Cheltenham, was reluctant to admit his guilt, but after nineteen hours of intensive questioning was persuaded to tell Cole the truth.

The extent of his treachery shocked the international intelligence community and it took five months to corroborate all the information contained in his confession. Prime has been described as the most important post-war KGB mole in British signals intelligence and Cole's investigation was publicly applauded by the attorney general, the late Lord Havers, who described it as 'masterly and remarkably diligent'. Unfortunately his involvement provided ammunition for those wishing to exploit a connection between the security services and the death of the relatively unknown, insignificant and elderly Hilda Murrell.

Dalyell questioned many aspects of the police investigation and fuelled more speculation. The connection between Cole and the security services was linked to the suspension of those detectives who chose to neglect work for a game of golf. Had they been given a nod and a wink to the effect that no conclusive result was required from the tasks allotted to them?

This continual pressure finally brought an official response. The chief constable, Robert Cozens, reacted angrily to the accusations against the integrity of his senior detective and acknowledged the effect of the adverse publicity on the nine-month-old inquiry. He publicly described Cole as an outstanding detective chief superintendent and acknowledged that the murder team had been distracted by having to research answers to satisfy the flood of speculation. More importantly, he considered it a distinct possibility that some witnesses had not come forward because of the continuing adverse comments. His message was clear – put up or shut up! It had some effect.

The police operation remained intense. Cole travelled daily the 120-mile return trip between Worcester and Shrewsbury. After fifteen months the long hours and pressure began to exact their toll and he took a holiday. The Dyfed Powis Constabulary allowed him facilities at Fishguard police station so that he could keep in touch with the incident room.

When he made contact Chris Furber was anxious to speak to him.

'You won't have seen the *Police Gazette* for last Wednesday: there's a photograph of a chap in custody in London for murdering two old ladies. I rang to get the details and they had something rather interesting to tell me.'

David McKenzie had been arrested for minor cases of arson, but eventually confessed to the murder in October 1984 of 76-year-old Barbara Pinder and nine months later to that of Henrietta Osborne, who was eighty-six.

Both women had endured terrible ordeals. Barbara Pinder was stabbed forty-five times with great ferocity, beaten and kicked in the head before being strangled with a single hand. Mrs Osborne, who was partially blind and deaf, was stabbed in the face and neck, her back had been broken and a ballpoint pen plunged into her neck. Before leaving the killer had placed her body on the bed and set light to it.

McKenzie's case was complicated by the fact that he also confessed to other murders, some of which he could not possibly have committed.

Furber's declared interest in the Murrell case stimulated the memory of the London detective to whom he had spoken.

'That's funny, guv – when we were taking him back to the cells after questioning one afternoon he said he attacked and badly injured an old lady some time last year when he was on his way to Wales to visit a cousin. He's as vague as that. I'm afraid he doesn't remember much about it at all.'

McKenzie had considerable psychiatric problems and a lengthy criminal record. A native of Dundee, he was living in London at the time of the Pinder and Osborne murders, but also wandered the country. Geography was not his strongest suit and he had little idea of the identity of places he visited. His mental problems manifested themselves in the cleansing of his soul to detectives: he explained his heart told him he was incapable of inflicting horrendous injuries on his victims, but his brain assured him he was. After making his confessions he would retract and convince himself of his innocence.

Warned that McKenzie was susceptible to suggestion, Cole and Furber approached him with extreme caution, not even mentioning Hilda Murrell by name. It is not unusual in any murder investigation for some individuals falsely to admit to the crime – one can never be sure of the motive. Usually they are eliminated, because they know nothing of the details of the crime and are quickly exposed by careful interrogation.

Although he claimed not to read newspapers or watch television, McKenzie said enough at his first interview with the West Mercia officers to justify an extensive inquiry into his movements during the days surrounding 21 March 1984.

What he did say was clouded by his alcohol-befuddled brain and gave the detectives little to go on. They were not the only ones who were confused by this complex man. At his first trial at the Central Criminal Court in May 1987 he pleaded guilty to the manslaughter of Pinder and Osborne on the grounds of diminished responsibility, but later withdrew those pleas and the issues proceeded to trial. After lengthy legal submissions he was declared unfit through mental disability to enter any plea and was sent to the secure hospital at Rampton.

In 1989 psychiatrists declared him fit enough to stand trial and January the following year found him back in the dock. The main issue again revolved around his mental condition. Six psychiatrists gave differing opinions about whether he was a fantasist or psychopath. It was all too much for McKenzie. He took himself off to the cells, telling Judge Kenneth Richardson that he found the evidence so upsetting he couldn't listen to any more.

On 1 February 1990 a jury found McKenzie guilty of manslaughter of the two elderly London ladies. He was remanded to a secure hospital once again. His confessions and conviction worried certain members of the legal profession but these were later relieved by the Appeal Court.

It was almost two years before Cole and Furber finished their enquiries about David McKenzie, during which time he was interviewed on several occasions. When they had taken the matter as far as they were able the Director of Public Prosecutions decided there was insufficient evidence upon which to base a charge.

The explanation for McKenzie's unprompted recollections of the Murrell saga and the environs of Shrewsbury, including the location of temporary traffic signals on the day of the murder, remains a mystery.

David McKenzie later successfully appealed against his conviction and was released. The Appeal Court judges were in effect setting a precedent for the future whereby a confession, uncorroborated by other evidence, would be inadequate to convict. The only evidence suggesting that he was in any way involved in the murder of Hilda Murrell came from McKenzie himself and, quite rightly, he was never charged or tried for the offence.

Cole has never spoken publicly about the investigation or his frustration at ill-informed comment and media hype, and he remains loyal to the efforts of those who are still trying to solve the mystery. He and Acland insist their summation of the circumstances will not be far from the mark when Hilda Murrell's killer is finally snared.

They harbour the hope that the DNA process of genetic fingerprinting will be further refined and developed so that it can be used to identify Hilda Murrell's killer from the traces of seminal fluid he left behind.

Although Acland had no such loyalties or pressures, he resigned from the University as he saw no quick resolution between his employers and the Home Office. He was forging a new career as an independent forensic pathologist. Like everyone involved he had been amazed at the level of interest and speculation. He was on the sidelines, an observer, until he noted that certain articles in the press were questioning aspects of the post mortem and impugning his impartiality. Why hadn't his report been released to the world at large? Why couldn't the relatives see the body? Why was there a second post mortem? Why was the funeral arranged so quickly after the body was released from the coroner's care?

Like Cole, Acland considered the best way to deal with the innuendoes was to meet them head-on. Unlike Cole, there was no one preventing him from doing what he wanted. But when he made phone calls to those in authority or with greater experience, who might give him advice, nobody wanted to know. He was on his own.

His decision was to write a letter to *The Times*. The reaction was explosive: an unused interview with Robin Day on Radio Four; an appearance on breakfast television; and a mention in *Private Eye*, which described him as pompous – a source of endless amusement to those who knew him. Granada TV questioned him for *World in Action*, taking twenty minutes to try to ascertain whether he thought the body had been moved after death. Each objection he raised to this view was countered by some procedure or precaution the assailant might have taken. Eventually he said, almost in desperation and with a touch of cynicism: 'Yes, if they moved the body, not disturbing the clothing or the hypostasis or rigor mortis [then it could be that the body had been moved].'

They only broadcast the last nine words! None the less it did the trick, at least as far as Acland was concerned. Hilda Murrell's family was invited to engage their own pathologist and Professor Bernard Knight reviewed the case. As a result of what he had to say no more accusations were heard about the veracity of the pathology, but the bandwagon of speculative and investigative journalism is difficult to stop once set in motion. Rumour fuels rumour as more individuals with vested interests leap upon the carousel.

There were so many inaccurate reports published about the circumstances of Hilda Murrell's violent end that any attempt to answer them fully would have filled volumes. But the chief constable, Robert Cozens, had one final try.

Given space in the local press under the headline 'THERE HAS BEEN NO COVER-UP' he attempted to answer the critics. A copy of the report Miss Murrell had compiled for the Sizewell inquiry was not missing; every one had been accounted for. The person who claimed her body was not in the copse on the

Thursday after her death could have been mistaken because of the area's topography. Sinister implications placed upon details of the burglar's search of the house and the degree of sexual activity were refuted. He gave precise reasons for the failure to find her body before the Saturday morning and for the employment of, till then, such little-used tactics as hypnosis and personality profiling during the investigation. But this attempt to quash the speculations had little effect. Cozens therefore considered it necessary to appoint an assistant chief constable from another police area to review the inquiry.

Peter Smith, an experienced detective from Northumbria, spent ten weeks on the task and was able to report in June 1985 that there was not one shred of evidence to link the crime with British intelligence services. He found nothing to support the political allegations, but described the murder as one of the most bizarre he had ever encountered. Smith's published opinion that Hilda Murrell's death was the tragic consequence of an opportunist burglary confirmed the conclusion reached by Cole and Acland months before.

The West Mercia Constabulary did not escape criticism, however. The failure to find the body until three days after death hampered the initial investigation and gave rise to much of the speculation. Smith was equally disapproving of the way the media had been handled and asserted that the immediate rebuttal of conjecture might have reduced its impact.

The only criticism he had of Cole's investigation was a failure positively to eliminate an unlikely suspect, whose name was put forward after he had committed suicide in East Anglia shortly after the murder. Smith discovered the suspect had been lunching with colleagues at the time of Miss Murrell's abduction about a hundred and fifty miles away. Cole had not taken matters that far. Having made enquiries into the initial information he had decided the possibility of a link was so tenuous as to make the deployment of further resources unnecessary. His judgement had proved right; he was paid to make such judgements and the criticism caused him no loss of sleep.

After ten years the killer is still at large but the hunt continues.

2 Arrogant Avarice

The Julia Avery Case

On a Monday morning in early February 1986 the telephone rang as Bernard Avery was leaving the house. He was surprised to hear his daughter's boyfriend, Mitch Robinson, on the line wanting to talk to him; they were not usually on speaking terms. Bernard knew that Robinson was in custody at Worcester police station on a robbery charge. He had pestered the station sergeant to let him make a telephone call before his 'father-in-law' left for work.

'I want to see Julia – I want her to bring Sophie down to see me. Can you call round on your way to work? You'll have to go round the back – she'll still be in bed and you won't wake her from the front door.'

Reluctantly Bernard agreed. He detested the arrogant young man who ill-treated his seventeen-year-old daughter and had precious little regard for other members of the family. But Bernard was a deeply religious man who preferred persuasion to confrontation; he always co-operated whenever he could.

He parked his car outside the terraced house in Tunnel Hill, on the northern fringe of Worcester city centre, and walked down the side alley. Hairs on the back of his neck stirred as he saw a hole in the glass near the handle of the back door. Something behind the door made it difficult for him to prise it open, and he squeezed himself through the gap into the kitchen calling out Julia's name. He went to the rear room and turned towards the stairs in the far corner. Now his hair stood on end as he saw Julia's naked body lying at the foot of the stairway. Her lifeless eyes stared at him like those of a discarded doll.

His horror stimulated panic and he fled to raise the alarm. As he waited for the police he dared not imagine what had happened to Julia's twelve-month-old baby.

Bernard's mind raced back to the events of the weekend. Julia was upset when told her boyfriend had been arrested for robbery. When he was brought to the house on Sunday morning by a couple of detectives she told lies to provide him with an alibi. After they left she turned to her parents for comfort and spent the day with them. She was little more than a child and the tempestuous relationship with Robinson had shattered her nerves.

Bernard had taken her home in the late evening and left with some reluctance. She had asked him to wait while she put the baby to bed and took her dustbin through the front door for collection next day.

'I've got to take it out the front, Dad. We haven't had a key to the back door since Mitch lost it.'

Her general unease did nothing to alleviate his sadness and concern.

'Mitch has got a lot of enemies. Everybody knows how strong he is and there's lots who are frightened of him. They know me too and might take it out on me when they know I'm on my own.'

Bernard would often reflect upon her prophetic final remark.

'If they come to get me they'll get through the back door. I can't come back home with you, Dad. Mitch might need me and he'd go mad if I wasn't here.'

Frustrated by his misguided daughter's logic, he drove away as she waved from the lounge window.

Constables Scott and Walters met Bernard at the front of the house and he stammered his fears for the baby as he described his grisly find.

Chris Walters stepped gingerly over the prostrate body, dreading what she might find upstairs. Pushing open a bedroom door she was greeted by the toddler's smiling face as she stood against the cot rails. The policewoman took off her coat and wrapped it tightly round the child, taking care to cover her face before going gingerly downstairs past Julia's prostrate form. She didn't stop to examine the chaotic scene in the bedroom next door to the child's.

There was no emotion or threatening outburst when a detective told Robinson that Julia was dead. He didn't ask how she had died or for any other details. His reaction was too contrived to be convincing – a moment's silence followed by: 'What do you mean? I only saw her Saturday. She's at home. I can't understand this. I can't believe it. Where's the baby? Can I have bail?'

Bernard Avery helped the police to piece together the last months of his daughter's life. He and his wife had adopted Julia and her older brother and sister. The children were brought up in the strict confines of a middle-class home, where the Christian faith dictated their lives. It was a severe disappointment when their son discovered social pleasures which flew in the face of their religious beliefs, and they viewed with equal alarm the tendencies of his impressionable kid sister to follow suit.

Julia was stubborn and hot-headed. She quickly discovered the clubs and pubs of the cathedral city were not frequented by dissipated, debauched demons but everyday, fun-loving kids like herself. In her *naïveté*, she was as a lamb to the slaughter, and was soon falling under the spell of the handsome, persuasive and charming Mitchell Robinson. He took no time at all to seduce her and, although horrified by the liaison, Bernard and his wife were powerless to do anything about it.

Mitchell Harding Robinson was contemptuous of most people unless he wanted favours. He learned to manipulate and take advantage of every situation at an early age. His quick wits and cunning were developed through fear of his deranged West Indian father who terrorized the family. Police were often called to the house and Robinson's attitude towards them was probably coloured by the sight of six officers struggling to subdue his father: he despised them.

When Robinson senior was committed to a secure mental institution Mitchell spent the remainder of his formative years in the care of foster parents and children's homes. There was little chance that the youth, with an increasingly large chip on his shoulder, would avoid continual brushes with the law.

Arrogance misled him into believing he had the perfect answer to evade his responsibilities: a combination of insolence and aggression. When arrested he only ever made one remark: 'I'm saying fuck all – you prove it.'

Quite often they couldn't and he would be released, reassured by his tactical success. On other occasions he would be detained as they tried to break his will. His reaction was equally predictable. 'If you think that'll work you can think again. I spent too much time as a kid chained in the shed like a dog to be frightened of being locked up.'

Robinson's relationship with Julia was always stormy and

her parents were unable to stop the violent outbursts. They received nothing but harassment if they raised any protest. Their daughter's inevitable pregnancy caused them considerable embarrassment but their Christian belief ensured continued support of the girl. Eventually the couple moved in together, but Julia frequently returned home battered and bruised. On one occasion Bernard and Olive arranged for her to spend time with a family friend, but Mitch only bullied other members of the family to disclose her whereabouts. It was during this period that Julia made a prophetic remark: 'I haven't got long to live. I just have a feeling.'

She was only seventeen years old.

During one separation, Mitch craftily enlisted the Social Services Department to help him gain access to his child. A meeting was arranged and the couple met on neutral ground in the company of Bernard Avery and a social worker. They listened to Robinson's hollow promises while Julia resisted his pleas for a reconciliation. Eventually, and inexplicably, she agreed to go for a ride in the country to discuss the future in private while Bernard stayed with the baby. Hours later he was summoned to the local hospital. Julia had been admitted following a road accident, and as she lay battered and bruised she told him she was returning to live with Mitch. Her decision was beyond his comprehension.

It would probably have been different if she had realized that during the drive Robinson tried to kill her. There were no seat belts in the car and he deliberately drove into a telegraph pole. While the girl was unconscious he tried to break her neck but was disturbed by a passing motorist who stopped to summon an ambulance. Julia placidly returned with him to the house where she was soon to meet her death.

Robinson didn't really want Julia. He was tired of her; she was an obstruction to his social life. He did however need his daughter, and needed Julia to care for her while he pursued his carefree lifestyle.

Robinson had a prodigious sexual appetite. A keep-fit fanatic, he had developed an impressive physique through regular body-building sessions. He worked regularly as a bouncer at local night clubs and seduced many of the young female clientele with charm and the promise of adventure. The number of his conquests was impressive. He often had sex with customers in unlikely places; on other occasions colleagues covered for his absence while he took girls home and performed on the marital bed when Julia was out. These naïve young women were oblivious to the ruthless, cunning nature of their Romeo.

Against this background, enquiries started into Julia's death.

David Cole looked round the narrow gap in the back door. There was glass on the floor from the shattered pane; on top of the shards lay a decorative house-brick. He noticed a key in the inside of the lock and, glancing through a side window into a rear room, saw Julia's body at the foot of the stairs.

He turned to a colleague. 'That brick's bone-dry – everything out here's sopping wet.'

A detective pushed some duckboards through the back door on to the kitchen floor and extended them towards the front room. Cole went into the kitchen and looked around with his hands stuffed deep in his pockets: an old habit to ensure he touched nothing. On a work surface he saw an identical brick to the one behind the door. Very odd. He walked along the boards into the rear room and that particular puzzle was solved. In the corner lay a pile of identical decorative bricks near a partially constructed fireplace. He muttered, to no one in particular, 'This is a bloody fit-up if ever I saw one.'

At the foot of the stairs the detective scanned Julia's body. A dark linear bruise surrounded the neck, blood seeped from an ear and he noticed the tell-tale signs of minute haemorrhages on the face. He was experienced enough to know how she had died, but Peter Acland's expert examination would, he hoped, tell him far more.

The pathologist arrived for his preliminary view. Each stage was photographed and large sheets of sticky tape were pressed against the flesh to pick up foreign hairs and fibres for future analysis. Then Julia was placed carefully into a plastic body bag which would also be minutely examined for similar debris once she had been removed.

With the stairway cleared, the pair visited the middle bedroom. Apart from the child's room it was the only one in a habitable state. The double bed was slewed drunkenly across the room; its base was fractured and a large amount of blood could be seen on the valance. Women's underwear was strewn about the floor and behind the door they found a distorted white leather belt. Peter Acland took a pair of tweezers from his pocket and picked up in turn a brassiere, pants and vest; they were all severely ripped.

'I shouldn't be surprised if this damage wasn't caused after they were removed from the body.'

There was something distinctly odd about the whole thing. Cole's initial assessment was being confirmed by the minute. He briefed 'Herbie' Perriton: 'Take this place apart, Herb – I don't mind how long it takes. It's got a story to tell.'

He did not need to say more; once a murder scene had been 'Perritonised' it would reveal no further secrets.

Acland's instincts were also telling him that 'not all was as it appeared' with this murder. The body had been easy to see through the back window, too easy to see – and perhaps that was the intention. The awkward position of the legs at the bottom of the stairs didn't quite fit with what one would expect from either falling back on to or down the staircase. They were uncovered and steep. At the bottom were three or four sheets of plywood propped against the wall. The severe, reddened abrasions round the neck, indicating the use of a broad ligature, were as striking as any he had seen. The entire face above the marks on the neck was covered by tiny pinpoint haemorrhages, characteristic of strangulation. But it was not just the obvious that cornered his attention; the obvious must only be accepted after a thorough examination to detect the obscure. He noted a small, dried trickle of blood from the right ear. This was not unusual in itself: deaths from various types of asphyxia are regularly associated with a little bleeding from the congested mucus membranes of the nose and ears.

'Nobody has moved anything, have they?'

He knew that in spite of the meticulous care of the investigating officers – and he always found the West Mercia officers meticulous – one could not always guarantee that a body hadn't been innocently moved after death. Relatives, ambulancemen, police surgeons – all might, for good reason, have disturbed it. In this case no one had since its discovery. Yet Acland saw that it had been moved since death, for the dried trail of blood from the right ear flowed upward, apparently defying gravity. She had been strangled face down or turned face down almost immediately and left like that long enough for a little blood to flow, dry and leave its clue.

Careful scrutiny at the mortuary revealed more information. The abrasive ligature marks merged into normal skin and at the junction there was an imprint of cloth. It was impressed into the abrasion and skin, just like marks left by tight elastic around the top of a sock. She was therefore still wearing her dressing-gown when she was killed. Furthermore, her body still bore the impression marks of her bra and pants.

'It seems as though she was strangled first and undressed afterwards.'

Cole tried to probe a little further. 'And this faint horse-shoe shaped mark on her chest, could it be a stomp with the heel of a shoe?'

'Oh, I wouldn't like to go that far; I'm wary of over-interpreting.'

However, as events turned out, the canny detective may well have been right.

Acland went on. 'It seems as though she had put up some sort of struggle. There's a long scuff mark to her right shin. She may have got that falling against the hard-edged base of her bed: And there's a couple of broken ribs on the left side of the chest ... a fall? a kick? a crush?'

The marks on the neck were carefully measured and scrutinized. Linear marks and interruptions suggested a broad ligature which had been twisted. Two 'ghost' abrasions adjacent to the main mark showed the ligature had been tightened twice and slipped before the main application. Two rounded red marks on the right front of the neck probably corresponded with some feature on the ligature. At the back it appeared to have been pulled in a downward direction on the right side and an upward direction on the left side.

The absence of certain features in the attack were to prove of equal importance to the investigation. There was no physical evidence of sexual interference as subsequent tests proved.

It was too early to reach firm opinions but Acland could confirm she had been strangled whilst wearing a dressing-gown, bra and pants. It had probably occurred in the bedroom and there had been a struggle: the bed was askew; she had an abrasion to her leg and two broken ribs; the ligature had to be applied two or three times; and then ... and then she had been moved; stripped of all clothing, moved along a narrow corridor, down steep stairs and placed on view from the rear window.

'Could one person carry her along such narrow passageways?'

'She hadn't been dragged. There aren't any marks in the dust on the floorboards. It would possibly be easier for two.'

Acland avoided offering an opinion on the time of death, but he knew he was going to be pushed. 'When was the last time that she was seen alive? What time was the body discovered?'

'9.45 p.m. last night and 9.45 a.m. this morning.'

His audience groaned as he confidently opined that she died somewhere between those times!

He was always wary of being dragged into an exercise of dubious precision. So many factors affect the calculations that they can easily be misleading. A time worked out on a wrong premise, or wrong information, may unduly influence the inquiry. Too narrow a range may wrongly implicate or wrongly eliminate suspects. He would only say she had been dead a few hours before discovery, but he wouldn't be pinned down within the twelve-hour period.

Later that evening, Cole and his deputy Allen Mayo met the detectives working on the case.

'He can say fuck all this time, Boss, because he couldn't have done it.'

The confident assertion was immediately countered. 'But I guarantee he had something to do with it.'

That seemed to be the opinion of the majority.

Robinson was a member of a group of fitness freaks. Some worked as night-club bouncers and spent their days in a gymnasium. They were in the main arrogant and dismissive of the normal rules of society. Among certain elements they strutted like turkey cocks, but no one with a brain gave them a second thought. However, they proved a considerable thorn in the side of the local police and were all difficult to deal with. Violence was their stock-in-trade and for some time they had been getting out of hand.

On the Saturday evening before Julia's death Robinson should have been on the door of Bobby McGee's basement bar in the city centre. He didn't turn up but arranged for someone to cover for him: Noel Brown, a huge illiterate youth whose only interests in life were fitness and the martial arts.

Robinson would arrive for duty at the Pavilion Club later in the evening, but first he had a score to settle. He decided to search the town for someone with whom he was looking to pick a fight. Johnnie Chadwick is a little cock sparrow of a man who had been unfortunate to involve himself in a business deal with Mitch. There was some ill-feeling between them about the settlement of a debt.

Johnnie sauntered into town early on Saturday evening; it was his birthday and he was intent on having a good drink. He made his way to Bobby McGee's where he thought he knew all the doormen, but didn't recognize the black youth standing at the top of the stairs. He knew the other one; Martin Evans was regularly there. The bar was almost deserted and he soon decided to move on, but as he reached the foot of the stairs he saw Mitch Robinson rushing towards him.

'What about my fucking money, Chaddie?' he shouted, aiming a blow at the little man's head. The scuffle was interrupted by Evans, who ushered the pair outside. Noel Brown helped Evans to restrain Robinson while Johnnie took to his heels and dived into a fish-and-chip shop. Robinson cornered him at the back of the shop and, in full view of staff and customers, gave him a severe beating. Afterwards Robinson calmly removed Chaddie's wallet from his pocket and left the shop, his shirt sleeve hanging in shreds from the little man's futile attempts to ward off the blows. Several people saw him making his way back to Bobby McGee's as an ambulance was called for his battered victim.

He handed the stolen wallet to Martin Evans. 'Here, give this back to your mate.'

He knew the police would soon be looking for him and didn't want to be in possession of incriminating evidence. He set off home to change his shirt.

Later in the evening, Robinson was arrested on the steps outside the Pavilion Club. Smartly dressed in evening suit and bow-tie he strutted confidently towards the police car winking at his young admirers on the pavement. His only comment to the arresting officer was entirely predictable: 'I'm saying fuck all.'

On Sunday morning Mitch was escorted home by detectives. He insisted on walking to the back of the house to tap on Julia's bedroom window. They found no sign of Chaddie's wallet or any other useful evidence and Julia told them Mitch had spent the evening with her before leaving for the Pavilion at about eleven o'clock. The young detectives did not press the issue; they knew the situation between the couple. She was obviously lying, but was clearly terrified to do otherwise.

Robinson returned happily to his cell. He knew the police would not release him on bail if he kept denying responsibility for the attack on Chadwick. He would be safely tucked up until Monday morning's court. This time he would really show these thick coppers – Mitchell Robinson would commit the perfect crime and they would be no match for his brilliance!

Early enquiries into Julia's death met with limited success. Julia's next-door neighbours had heard a loud crash followed by a prolonged disturbance in the bedroom at about half-past one on Monday morning. They were used to the sounds of the young girl being abused but this row beat them all. There were no voices, but the crashing around went on for ten or fifteen minutes. It sounded as if Robinson had taken it into his head to knock a wall down in the dead of night. It was not unusual for the arrogant and aggressive young man to give little thought for his neighbours. He intimidated them and they were wary of complaining.

Four doors away another neighbour was just going to bed at half past one when she heard glass breaking and men's voices. She thought someone was stealing the family car, and insisted her husband went to check. The car was all right and he went back to bed.

Enquiries had been made about Mitch's associates. If Cole was right and Robinson was involved, the conspiracy would more than likely be with someone he knew. The coincidence of a random killing was too much to stomach, particularly since he and Acland were convinced that the forced entry and sex attack were both contrived.

Detective Constables Mark Smythe and Lee Mullen had some information. Both were local lads who had grown up alongside many of their clientele.

'You might be interested, Boss. One of the bouncers from Bobby McGee's was in the nick at teatime. I wanted to see him about the robbery. When I spoke to him he got all nasty and rushed out through the door. After I caught up with him and told him I only wanted to ask him a few questions about the robbery he calmed down. I've known him all my life and never had any reaction like that. He said he'd come in to see how Mitch was, but I can't think why he triggered off.'

A voice interrupted him. Derek Griffin, an exceptionally astute detective sergeant reaching the end of his service, had been a personal friend and confidant of Cole's for many years. He knew everything that was worth knowing about Worcester.

'He's not the only one on edge. Everybody connected with Robinson is either running around the city like headless chickens or we can't find 'em. We don't need to look far, Boss, but they're good at keeping quiet. What we've got to do first is make sure Robinson don't get bail – if he gets on the outside nobody'll say anything for fear of a hiding.'

The evidence on the robbery was watertight and Cole anticipated no difficulty in obtaining a remand to custody when Robinson came before magistrates the following day. However, he knew enough about the vagaries of the courts not to put his shirt on it.

Early on Tuesday morning the chief superintendent visited the murder scene for an update from Herbie Perriton. As they stood in the rear yard swapping theories Bernard Avery arrived. He obviously wanted to tell them something about Julia's death, but his mild personality and strong beliefs caused him to wrestle with his conscience. He was reluctant to point the finger at anyone. He talked of the Christian spirit of forgiveness and amazed his listeners with his composure. Although clearly devastated by Julia's death, he could not bring himself to condemn the man who had caused his family so much aggravation.

Finally, he blurted out: 'I thought you chaps ought to know. I've been told Mitch has taken out huge insurance on Julia's life recently.'

It was the motive they were looking for. Herbie set about finding the policies.

Cole hurried away to another murder inquiry and in mid afternoon was in the other incident room when he received a telephone call. The magistrates had bailed Robinson. In an impassioned plea his solicitor had spoken of his devastation at Julia's death and the need to arrange for the welfare of the infant daughter. The local evening paper showed him leaving the court grinning his head off.

But the contingency had been catered for. Detectives were waiting to put a tail on him. Within hours he visited his home. He demanded access – he wanted clothing for himself and the baby. The policeman guarding the door barred his way as Robinson threatened, bullied and abused.

Herbie Perriton handed him some clothes through the front door. It was the kind of co-operation he could well do without. The insurance policies were inside and he wanted them, although he dare not say so. He was already too late. Herbie had found them in a drawer and they were now with Cole.

The following morning an insurance representative told detectives that Robinson had visited the office several times in recent weeks seeking reassurance about the cover extended by the policy on Julia's life. The last time had been the previous Saturday morning when he arrived with an attractive young female. It was not Julia.

Another company had issued a policy within months of the girl's death. In total, Robinson had covered her life for £150,000. Given that he was unemployed and continually hard-up, the money required to service the policies was suspiciously excessive, but they were always fully paid.

On Wednesday morning Mitch was observed visiting the insurance offices. He wanted to know when he would be paid out. Julia had been murdered only three days before!

Over the next couple of days detectives interviewed Robinson's associates. Other officers who followed him watched incredulously as he escorted young females on shopping expeditions and around pubs and clubs. He spent the night with one in a friend's flat on the Thursday, and on Friday he and another friend slept with a couple of girls in a city flat. Everyone seemed to regard him as a bit of a hero.

The main reason for his release on bail received little attention; Sophie had been dumped on a friend and forgotten.

Cole was in his office early on Thursday morning. When senior members of his team arrived they found him in shirt sleeves, shrouded in a cloud of smoke. It was always a sure sign that the pressure was on when he resorted to the foul-smelling pipe first thing in the day. Supplied with a constant stream of black coffee, he was reading all the statements taken over the previous days and scribbling notes on scraps of paper.

No one interrupted him until Mayo asked: 'The briefing's due in a couple of minutes. Are you coming down?'

'No, you take it this morning. I'm doing a bit of thinking. When you come back I'll tell you who killed her.'

The optimistic remark was said with some conviction and his friend knew better than underestimate the possibility. But it was not to prove so easy.

When Mayo returned the office was deserted. A note lay on the table: 'It's going to take a bit longer than I thought. Gone home to get away from the phones. See you at 8.30 tomorrow –

get the team leaders together in the briefing room.'

Half a dozen senior detectives sat round a table. David Cole held the floor as he went through his research of the previous twenty-four hours. His wife had most reason to regret his sleepless night; his study adjoined their bedroom and the light had blazed through the glass-panelled door most of the night.

'I haven't come up to expectations – I don't know who strangled Julia Avery! But I do know Mitchell Robinson is behind it. I'm sure the murderer isn't very far away. It will be someone within his immediate circle. He hasn't got the brains or contacts to hire a professional killer. Neither has he got the money. No professional's going to bump her off on the promise of an insurance payout. He'd want a lot of money up front.'

His main concern was the silence they were meeting, but he knew the reason for it. While Mitchell Robinson was on the streets people were frightened to talk.

Cole continued. 'All you've given me so far is the suspicion and innuendo of a conspiracy. I need to lock him up and keep him locked up, and I need evidence if I'm going to do it. The evidence has got to be good enough to make sure he stands on a charge far more serious than the robbery on John Chadwick.'

The meeting discussed and dissected every piece of information at hand. They agreed to continue probing Robinson's background and activities in the hope someone would break.

The little bit of luck that is always required came later in the day. A woman telephoned; she had been told Mitchell Robinson had offered a friend a considerable sum of money in recent months in return for the disposal of Julia. She was able to name names.

After thirty-six hours of careful planning, nine people were arrested in a co-ordinated swoop at seven o'clock on the following Sunday morning. Among them was Mitchell Robinson. Teams of officers interviewed the suspects while others searched their homes. More detectives concentrated on the people with whom Robinson had been seen to socialize since his release from custody.

On Monday Cole was far from despondent. He prepared to release most of those detained while he made more enquiries. He was not ready to give Robinson his freedom and had just about enough evidence to hold him.

One of the prisoners said he had been offered money to kill Julia, but thought it was a joke. Another told of a conversation

with Robinson about the commission of a 'perfect crime'. He
had said the criminal would be untouchable if he could make
sure he was in police custody when the crime was actually
committed.

Information from another source said that Robinson and a
young girl visited shops in Redditch, twenty miles from
Worcester, on the day before Julia's death and purchased a
balaclava helmet, woollen gloves and a pair of training shoes.
The identity of the girl was not yet known, but a till receipt on
Julia's dressing-table confirmed the purchases.

Robinson was charged with conspiracy to murder and
remanded into custody. He missed his freedom and instructed
his solicitor to fight for his release on every possible occasion.
The eloquence of his advocate was stretched to the limits as he
made continual complaints to magistrates at remand hearings
in the following weeks about the lack of evidence against his
client. His spleen was directed towards the police and their
failure to charge the actual murderer.

'The public has a right to know what progress is being made
... the state of that progress ... is zero. The police are
scrummaging around ... they are whistling in the dark.'

He was entitled to his opinion and in one respect was bang
on target: the police were scrummaging around. But they were
not whistling in the dark; progress was steadily being made.
They were unlikely at that stage to confide the fact to anyone.

With Robinson tucked away, the evidence against him was
easier to obtain. On the day he was released from police
custody he bragged about his part in the plot to two friends, but
did not identify the murderer. No one could be in any doubt
about his relief at being rid of Julia. Not only had he pressed
insurance companies for immediate honouring of the payment;
he also borrowed £200 to buy one of his girlfriends a simulated
fur coat.

While the evidence mounted against Robinson the identification of Julia's killer was proving more difficult. The scientists
had confirmed that the white leather belt found in the bedroom
was the ligature, and that the blue fibres found on it came from
the gloves Robinson had bought the day before her death.

But who was it who had actually wrapped the belt round the
girl's neck?

Cole was constantly reminded of the solicitor's jibe that he was whistling in the dark as he sat for hour after hour examining documents and directing more and more extended enquiries to try and reach a breakthrough. He knew he was on the right track; all he needed was the lever to prise the case open.

After two weeks they got nowhere and Mayo was getting frustrated. 'Do you know how many jobs Spud Taylor has identified from that single inquiry you gave him yesterday? 682. If we go on like this we'll soon have enough work for a couple of years and there's no certainty it'll take us any further. That bloody computer will keep churning work out but we'll be getting nowhere. We've got to have a reassessment.'

It was another long session. In the early hours of the morning they made up their minds on which way they would go.

'We've been right all day. The answer lies in that small group. Instead of us trying to find out everything about them, let's try a different tactic. We'll make sure they tell us something about themselves. Stop that machine spewing out any more rubbish – everybody we've got available is going to go undercover.'

They were going to start creeping around the dusky world of local criminality, concentrating on unnerving those closest to Robinson by collecting evidence in order to have them arrested for offences they had been suspected of committing in the past. They received attention from the time they left their houses until they were put to bed at night.

An initial customer was a wild young man who thought he was above the law and saw no need to conform to the requirements of orderly society. His ambitions in life revolved around sex and violence. The observers quickly formed a profile of his routine and obtained enough evidence to arrest him several times in the space of a few days. Eventually he tired of the attention and was the first to crack. Robinson had offered him money to take part in a plot to kill Julia. He knew about the earlier attempt on Julia's life when she had been tricked into the car ride and finished up in hospital. Robinson had told him how he tried to break her neck while she lay unconscious at the kerbside. He was totally indifferent towards her. 'You'd never believe how hard it is to break somebody's neck,' he had said.

The wayward youth kept the information to himself until the pressure of continual police attention finally broke his will.

Even he could not identify Julia's eventual killer and Cole directed his attention towards another of Robinson's associates.

The need for vigorous surveillance came to an abrupt end within hours of the next target operation swinging into action.

As part of his strategy Cole had deployed detectives among their criminal informants. It gradually bore fruit. In any community there are always people involved with the criminal fraternity who are prepared to tell tales. They do so for a variety of reasons – some to ingratiate themselves, others in anticipation of favours, and quite a proportion do so for monetary advantage. Whatever the reason for betraying their associates informants are a most dangerous breed and many detectives have come to grief through handling them carelessly. David Cole always practised and taught the maxim that the detective controls the informant, not the other way round. It was a philosophy which would stand him in good stead in the weeks following Julia's death.

A few days after her murder, a local newspaper quoted a police spokesman as complaining about the dearth of information reaching the investigators. It was apparent things were being kept very tight. Cole still did not believe that either Robinson or any of his associates had the money, or connections, to bring in a professional. They were all small-town nonentities, whose world horizons only went as far as two weeks on the Costa del Sol. If he was right and kept his nerve, some information would bubble to the surface. He did not have to wait long for an initial contact.

Detective Sergeant Derek Griffin was passing through the foyer of Worcester police station one Saturday lunchtime at the end of February when he saw someone he knew standing at the enquiry desk. Derek passed the time of day and the visitor eagerly responded. He clearly wanted to talk about the Avery murder but was evasive and obviously on a 'fishing' expedition. The detective was having none of it; in his usual forthright manner he told him to stop beating about the bush and come out with what he wanted.

The young man had been on the receiving end of police tactics in the past and thought himself something of an expert. Allegedly he had worked out what the investigation was costing the constabulary and believed he would save them money if he could establish the killer's identity for them. It was a business proposition that was completely devoid of any sentimentality over Julia's death. He mentioned the amount he was looking for and Griffin burst into laughter:

'Look, my old son, anything above a fiver is beyond me – you're talking to the wrong bloke. I've never heard of that amount being paid to anybody. I reckon you'd better come back when you know something concrete and speak to the Gaffer.'

A few days later he was back, wanting to speak to Roger Morris, the detective chief inspector. Morris knew that he associated with some of the individuals who had featured in the inquiry and was interested to hear what he had to say. Morris also knew that if anyone in the city was likely to know the killer's identity it would be the man sitting in front of him. The bargaining started.

For several weeks a cat-and-mouse situation developed: the informant teased with snippets of information and Morris, waiting to pounce, negotiated patiently. Morris knew to whom he was talking, as did Cole, and both men had a fair idea that perseverance would pay dividends.

Eventually it did: the informant realized he was not going to secure a football-pools-sized payout, but was anxious to retain interest in his proposition. Morris delivered Cole's ultimatum:

'You can have thirty per cent of what you originally asked for in return for the killer's identity and evidence to convict him. You've already said enough to satisfy us you know who he is.'

The bait was taken and he quickly confirmed he knew the assailant's identity.

Morris listened intently: then came the crunch. 'How do you know – how do I know it's not a load of old cobblers?'

'He told me himself.'

'Well, that makes you a witness.'

The look on the informant's face told Morris such a possibility had not occurred to him.

'All right, Mr Morris, I'll be straight with you. He didn't say it to me, he told a friend of mine who doesn't want to get involved.'

Morris played along and told him he would need more detail as well as a name before anyone could be arrested on his say-so. He was hardly out of the office before the detective was on the telephone to Cole. 'Softly, softly catch a monkey, Roger,' said his boss. 'He wants the money, he'll be back.'

A few hours later Cole and Allen Mayo discussed the

stalemate over a pint. The killer's tracks had been well covered, and they were all too well aware of the reluctance of any associate of Robinson to assist. The informant was the best break they had so far. But if indeed he knew of the killer's identity only through an intermediary they were not much further forward in terms of evidence. The only avenue left was to take over the negotiations themselves.

At the arranged meeting Mr X, as he was thereafter known, misread the situation in thinking his valuable knowledge gave him the privilege to dictate proceedings. He was keen to make an impression as a macho man with a hold over the local underworld.

Within seconds Cole had heard enough and, in the language of the streets, put the position in perspective.

'Don't give me that bollocks. This place ain't big enough for an undervillage, let alone an underworld. In my opinion there's no one here bigger than a fucking two-bob bit and round here it's my opinion that counts. Now let's talk turkey. You want money. You know how much you can have. I want to convict the killer of a young girl. You say you've been talking to a friend – it's important he comes forward.'

Cole's fingers had been tapping the blotter in front of him and the informant's eyes were drawn towards it. On the blotter was a photograph of himself talking to another man. It had been taken a few days previously by a surveillance team. Cole looked him full in the eyes; the sweat started to drip from the informant's forehead and off the end of his nose.

Taken off guard he started to stammer his demands until Cole held up his hand.

'Thanks – you've just identified your friend.'

'Watcha mean?'

'You just used his Christian name as you were rambling on. That's him in the photograph.'

There was no reaction, just a commitment to try and persuade the friend to come forward.

As Mr X left the station two scruffy-looking characters in leather jackets and jeans hopped into an old banger and slotted into the traffic behind his car. Further along the street, tucked away in side streets, three similar vehicles waited to take their turn. The Regional Crime Squad Surveillance Unit was at work.

They followed closely as he hurriedly visited two business premises and a health club. He appeared to speak to no one until he drew up outside a house undergoing renovation. His friend was working inside and they went into a huddle.

In the early evening the telephone rang in Cole's office.

'There's a Mister Evans at the front desk asking to see you, sir.'

The clean-cut, impressively fit and muscular young man was shown into the senior investigator's office. He was prepared to tell Cole and Mayo about a conversation he had had with Noel Brown on the evening Julia's body was discovered. Brown, one of the group of men who had been arrested shortly after the murder, told him he had killed Julia. Although he was now prepared to grass his friend he was not willing to commit himself to a written statement or give evidence against him at court.

The detectives faced an impasse. They were told that anything which might have borne forensic traces had been destroyed. Brown had said, when interviewed earlier, that he had not moved from his flat on the Sunday night, a story which could be neither corroborated or contradicted. It was an uncomplicated, easily assimilated, alibi and even the dullard Brown was unlikely to be tripped up on its detail. Independent evidence was a necessity; and Evans was the key if he had received a detailed account of the commission of the crime.

Evans was no lover of the police and made his dislike plain. He was not overawed or impressed by rank and spoke freely of his distrust of detectives. He had already been questioned on several occasions about his association with Robinson and his dealings with John Chadwick's wallet. His movements on the weekend of the murder had been scrutinized, his family and girlfriend closely questioned. It was perhaps no wonder that his views towards the police were jaundiced.

They spoke for over two hours. Each time it was suggested that a note should be taken for the sake of accuracy Evans threatened to leave. They could not afford to lose him because he was telling them all they wanted to know. The notes would have to come later.

Noel Brown told Evans everything when he visited the flat and now, several weeks later, he could confirm everything the detectives had deduced from their own enquiries. The young black man worshipped Evans as a father figure, a reward for sympathy and support when the youngster's dim wits made him the object of ridicule.

Brown had pleaded: 'You won't tell anyone will you, Martin?'

Until now Evans had not let him down.

Evans account threw up a multitude of questions. 'You've got a daughter yourself – how could you keep this quiet until now? ... You come from a good family. What's this going to do to them? ... Why did you stick with Mitch Robinson when he was on bail if you knew he'd recruited young Noel to kill his missus?'

While admitting to sleepless nights wrestling with his conscience and worrying about the effect on his family, he nevertheless refused to accept he had a civic duty to turn his friend in. Evans blamed the police for everything. Their tactics had been wrong. They should not have made themselves so busy. It had made everybody jumpy about being implicated. The two older men listened impassively. They were accustomed to amateur detectives who always knew better than the professionals. While the young man was prepared to continue talking they were certainly patient enough to tolerate his arrogance. The discussions got nowhere, however, and finally Cole told Evans bluntly either to commit himself to a written statement or he would obtain a court order to ensure he gave evidence. This possibility had escaped Evans and he asked for time to consider the situation, he would go home and sleep on it.

The next morning Cole discussed tactics with his colleague. They had made a careful note of everything Evans told them. Every piece of detail had to be analysed to establish the next step in the inquiry if he failed to return. They both knew that the threat to summon him before a court was an empty one; no one can be forced to talk if they don't want to. If Noel Brown was interviewed again and maintained his original story any move they made now would be of crucial importance. Their difficulties did not concern them for much longer.

Shortly after eleven Roger Morris rang. He had received a telephone call; a man said Noel Brown wanted to give himself up. Martin Evans and a friend had spoken to Brown and convinced him that he should surrender. Morris, not surprisingly, had been taken aback by the information.

'You'd better come in here and see what my gaffer's got to say about this.'

Cole was not amused. Warning bells started to ring. If the two men had taken the law into their own hands and put pressure on Brown it was likely his confession would be worthless. What they had done could destroy six weeks' painstaking work. As Mayo drove him into Worcester Cole sucked his pipe and quietly fumed.

The caller was ushered into Cole's office; he was breathless as they shook hands. 'Sorry I'm a bit excited, but I've just cleared up a murder, know what I mean?'

'What I know is you've probably fucked it up completely.'

The amateur detective looked incredulous at this lack of appreciation as Cole told him in simple terms exactly where he had gone wrong. 'If you've laid a finger upon that lad I'll throw the bloody book at you. Any admission he made to you would be useless. You'd better tell me everything that's happened.'

Brown had been taken from his flat that morning and driven to a nearby car park. He was persuaded to give himself up to relieve the intense pressure the police were putting on others to break the wall of silence. It was the burden he had placed on his mentor, Martin Evans, by telling him about the killing, which tipped the scales.

Cole could not be sure about the story until he saw the youth himself. 'Where is Brown now? I want to speak to him.'

'He's settling his affairs – he'll be here at one o'clock.'

When Brown surrendered he admitted killing Julia and sat with his solicitor calmly telling the gory story. He implicated Robinson, who, he said, had planned the whole affair and bullied him to kill Julia. The picture seemed complete.

Then, weeks later, the hand of Mitchell Robinson intervened again. He obviously got to know that Brown had put him in the frame for murder. He was not amused and asked to see a detective.

'I'm bollocksed on the murder and the conspiracy, ain't I? But I ain't taking it on me own. You get Mayo and I'll spill the beans.'

Allen Mayo, who had interviewed Robinson on several occasions and established a rapport, hurried to the cells to speak with Robinson's solicitor. The poor man was being given the run-around by his client. Sometimes he seemed to accept advice, only to ignore it shortly afterwards. Sometimes he wanted the lawyer present when he was being interviewed and on others showed him the door.

In unguarded moments Robinson confided in his police escorts: 'I don't know where the hell I am. Joe [his solicitor] tells me to do one thing, then Mayo says another. What am I going to do?'

The listeners knew his reputation and without hope of

success casually remarked: 'All you can do, Mitch, is tell the truth and get it over with. That's all anybody wants.'

It was too much to hope. He was as crafty as a cartload of monkeys. He made a statement implicating others in the plot to kill Julia, but Cole and Mayo were not prepared to take anything he said at face value. They were certainly too long in the tooth to take any action on such a statement without careful examination, and many months of enquiry followed the new revelations. Brown, in the isolation of his cell, had plenty of time to reflect on his predicament. Eventually he also asserted that he had not been alone at the time of Julia's death.

The outcome of this intense activity was a trial at Birmingham Crown Court involving three men charged with murder: Brown, Robinson and Martin Evans. It was a messy business. Intrigue, sordid sex and unbridled violence exposed over the six week trial titillated a voracious press. The reports shocked many in the respectable shire city who were quite unaware that activities usually associated with the 'red light' areas of larger conurbations had occurred in their midst.

Noel Brown pleaded guilty and was removed from the court to a remand centre while the trial of his co-accused continued. He would later give evidence against them and needed to be isolated for his own protection.

Martin Wilson QC took the jury through the case. It was gruesomely simple. A murder had been staged to look like a burglary and frenzied sexual attack. So violent was the attack that the main strut on the base of the victim's bed had been broken. Julia's body was stripped and her underclothes torn before she was placed at the foot of the stairs. The killer's *coup de grâce* was to stamp on her neck to make sure it was broken. Neighbours testified to breaking glass, fifteen minutes of violence and male voices. The botched job had been done for an insurance pay-out and it was the Crown's case that it had been engineered by Robinson and Evans and executed by Evans and Brown.

The first witnesses spoke of Robinson's attempts to recruit someone to kill Julia. A succession of pretty young girls told of sex sessions with him in the days immediately before and after Julia's death. One of them had been given a fur coat purchased with £200 that he borrowed in the week following the murder. Another had married just before the trial and her husband knew nothing about her involvement.

The jury sat through Noel Brown's evidence. Showing

obvious signs of discomfort he went through each chilling detail. On the Saturday evening Mitchell Robinson had handed him the clothes he was to wear and the key to the back door. He set his alarm for one o'clock on Sunday morning and claimed that he met Evans outside Julia's house. He didn't want to go through with the plan but had been forced to do so.

Not unexpectedly, he was subjected to a most rigorous cross-examination by Counsel for both his co-accused. He did not budge from his story, and no one watching his ordeal could be under any illusion that the lad was dim-witted and immature and that he had been deceived by those he regarded as friends.

Mitchell Robinson spent a long time in the witness box. He arrogantly played to the gallery, the jury and anyone else whose attention he could attract. Throughout four days he faced intense questioning by his own lawyer and severe cross-examination from those representing Brown and Evans. His ego was only briefly deflated by a rebuke from the judge when he was caught grinning broadly as details of the murder were discussed.

His defence was simple: he wasn't there – he couldn't have been there – he was in custody – he knew nothing about any plans to kill his girlfriend. He did not find it so easy to explain why he had made a statement involving the others. Ingeniously he tried to make the jury believe that his false statement had been made to show how easy it was for innocent men to be charged. He vainly hoped it would convince them of his own innocence.

Evans also spent four days in the witness box. He told the jury that Brown had admitted to being the killer within twenty-four hours of Julia's death. At first he had not believed the story but realized the awful truth when the facts coincided with details supplied by the newspapers. Misguided loyalty had prevented him from going to the police for five weeks, but when pressure built up on so many of his family and friends he persuaded Brown to give himself up.

Although Robinson had offered him £40,000 to kill Julia some months before her death he had not taken the proposition seriously and claimed that he found himself in the dock because Brown had turned against him. Once again he blamed the police's putting pressure on the murderer as the reason for his friend's false betrayal.

The jury took its time to reach a verdict. After an overnight adjournment they emerged from their room at lunchtime the next day. A packed court waited with bated breath as the foreman provided a touch of light relief:

'Mr Foreman of the Jury, have you reached a verdict upon which you are all agreed in respect of any of the accused?'

'No.'

'A woman sitting next to him anxiously tugged his jacket and whispered in his ear. 'Oh, yes we have – Robinson's guilty.'

Back they trooped to their room to deliberate about Martin Evans. Two hours later they were unable to reach a verdict, and the judge ordered a retrial.

Mr Justice Boreham took little time in sentencing the two guilty men. Brown got life without a recommendation on how long he should serve. He was too young for such a consideration. Robinson was not so fortunate.

'You are a cruel, calculating, cynical manipulator and I recommend you should stay in prison for twenty years.'

There was still a cynical grin on his face as he turned on his heel and disappeared down the dock steps.

Mr Justice Boreham had not quite finished: 'Are Cole and Mayo in court? I have something I wish to say to them if they will come to the well of the court.

'I speak to you as representing all your squad, do you understand? Throughout this inquiry you faced a dreadful wall of silence. I am experienced enough to know what that meant. You faced appalling difficulties before your persistence successfully penetrated it. The public owes you a debt of gratitude.'

It was a good note to end on.

As he left the court Cole was approached by a senior lawyer. 'Your bravest move was the dragnet when you pulled so many in at the start. It isolated the organizer. You didn't have much evidence to go on but it did the trick. Well done.'

The detective silently agreed.

Some months later Martin Evans was acquitted of murder. He then pleaded guilty to a charge of attempting to pervert the course of justice in relation to his involvement with John Chadwick's wallet. He was sentenced to nine months' imprisonment but the length of time he had spent in gaol awaiting trial meant that he walked from the Court a free man.

3 Mindless Violence

The Carol Martin Case

In the middle of the afternoon a piercing scream echoed through the concrete maze of a multi-storey car park. It continued, some said, for thirty seconds or a minute, although Peter Acland would later say that a continuous human scream is unlikely to last for longer than ten seconds. However long it took, no one did anything. Many people did nothing, they later said, because they thought the noise was children larking about.

The extensive Redditch shopping centre serves the population of the burgeoning overspill town and attracts customers from a wide area. The shopping malls are reached by lifts and staircases leading from car parks surrounding the central spine. It is always busy. With continual movement of traffic and pedestrians it is remarkable that no one witnessed the tragedy enacted on level 8 of car park 2.

Within a couple of minutes of the shrill cries a vehicle descended the ramp from the floor above and turned into level 8's central aisle. In front the couple in the car, Mr and Mrs Underwood, saw a bundle of clothing obstructing their path – then, with a second glance, saw it was a human form.

Stunned into a moment's immobility they saw a young man walk from the shadows on their left, bend over the body and beckon them towards him. Graham Underwood walked a few feet forward. Then he saw blood, pools of it, staining the floor.

'We'll go for help.'

Shortly afterwards the couple reached the exit: 'There's been a bad accident on level 8. It looks like a young lad's been knocked over. There's blood all over the place. We left another young chap with him.'

The attendant reached for a telephone linking him with the security office and the couple gratefully drove away. Their parking ticket, stamped with precise entry and exit times, joined hundreds already lying in the till. They called at the nearby police station to ensure that the alarm had been raised: no one asked their name or any questions about their experience.

Security guards found a youth kneeling beside the stricken form of a young woman; she was in a desperate state and they were helpless. A young policeman arrived and she tried to tell him something but no sound would come. The woman had been cut, very, very badly, all over her body and face – this was no accident. By the time the ambulancemen arrived she was dead.

Personal radio sets started to crackle and within minutes the area was sealed off. Cars which continued to descend towards the exits had a long wait as detectives organized themselves to question everyone.

David Cole and Peter Acland were in the autopsy room at Worcester's Ronkswood Hospital. They were halfway through the examination of another murder victim when the telephone rang.

A scientific officer called out, 'Headquarters control room for you, Gaffer.'

In flat and factual tones the voice spelled out the message. 'Suspicious death at Redditch, sir: female, town centre car park, found about half an hour ago.'

Cole uttered a mild expletive. He was committing a sizeable proportion of his resources to finding the killer of the eighteen-year-old girl on the slab behind him. Clutching at straws, he asked the obvious question:

'What do you mean by "suspicious"?'

There was good reason for the question: he knew he would not have been told if it had been a straightforward traffic accident, but several times each month he and Acland were called to view deaths for which there was no ready explanation. The majority resolved themselves innocuously. This time they were not so fortunate.

'I'm told it looks like a stabbing – no immediate suspect.'

Two murders within the space of six hours, neither of which readily resolved, as is the case with eighty-five per cent of homicides. He had no option but to delegate the second to a colleague.

'Will you have a look at another on your way home, Peter? I've told them not to move the body – it's in a car park.'

The police surgeon certified death with minimum disturbance of clothing, but recoiled from the ferocity of the wounds. His diagnosis set in motion a search for a weapon, whilst the area around the victim was made sterile until the arrival of scientists and photographers. Hapless motorists, innocently trapped in the confusion, waited to be released from the concrete labyrinth as police officers recorded their names before directing them to the exits through a maze of pillars, and away from a view of the tragedy.

In the commotion two things appeared isolated and ignored: in a taped enclosure the shapeless form which had once been Carol Martin, and a quivering Stuart Hopkins sitting in a police car with a sympathetic ambulance attendant for company. A young detective spoke to him:

'You the lad who found her?'

'I just saw her lying there and I was going for help but then I heard another car coming down the ramp, so I ran out to stop it. The other people said they'd go and I stayed with her. Can I go home now?'

The eyes behind the thick spectacles were shifting from the detective's piercing gaze. After a while the officer returned with the police surgeon. 'We'd best get you away from here. You can tell us all about it at the police station.'

'What about my car?'

'It can't be moved at the moment. We'll look after it.'

Carol Martin had everything to live for: a successful husband; two children; a house in the picturesque village of Inkberrow, mythical setting of the Archers' Ambridge; good looks; health and bubbly personality. Everyone she knew adored her, but they also knew the limits of their relationship. She expected the same standards from friends as she insisted upon from her family. No one took advantage of Carol Martin or behaved improperly in her presence without being made aware of her displeasure. It may have been these character traits which led to her death.

On Monday 3 February 1986 she left just enough time to visit the shops before collecting the children from school – her movements were accurately timed by receipts found in her purse.

At 2.32 p.m. Carol removed a parking ticket from the machine and drove to level 8. Dressed in a tracksuit and trainers the ordinary, unremarkable shopper hurried towards the lifts, blonde, coiffured hair swinging in time with her steps.

Quick visits to the building society, Boot's and Sainsbury's. Then back to the car. She unlocked the driver's door and placed her bag on the seat when something attracted her attention. The car door remained ajar and an arc of blood led to the centre of the gangway where she died.

What distracted her? Was it an unseen and unprovoked frenzied attack or had she reacted against an offensive approach? No one will ever know; the only certainty was the final outcome: Carol never reached her children.

A searching policeman found a blood-stained knife blade in a gutter on a lower level; later its matching handle was discovered on the flat roof of an adjacent building fifteen feet above level 8. The void between the two buildings and the overhanging buttresses of the car park made it difficult to imagine how it reached the roof. The lighter blade did not traverse the divide and had fluttered downwards to the gutter. It needed no Holmesian detective to associate the discoveries with Carol Martin's murder. Carefully photographed, the pieces were gingerly placed in two sterile plastic containers.

Hopkins's myopic gaze shifted away from a direct encounter with the eyes of his questioner. He was calmer now, warmer and comfortably seated in an office at the police station.

He was required to remember everything about his day. Minor details might seem unimportant to him, he was told, but could eventually be connected with what others would say and help to build a complete sequence of events. Did he understand? A nod was the only answer.

Stuart Hopkins was nineteen and studying for A levels at a local college. He had attended lectures during the morning and at lunchtime decided to go for a drive. He had recently passed the driving test and needed all the practice he could get. When he returned for the afternoon session he couldn't find a parking space at the college so went to level 8 on car park 2.

He had some free time and thought that if he walked round the shops for a while the parking situation might have eased

when it was time to return to his studies. On making his way
back to the car he discovered Carol Martin. Thinking he had
come across a road accident victim he went to her aid, but
when he saw the blood he felt helpless and had no idea what to
do. She was trying to tell him something as he knelt beside her.
Cradling her head in his arms his sense of helplessness
intensified, so he decided to go for assistance.

He reached his car a few yards away and had just opened the
door when he heard another vehicle coming down the ramp
from the floor above. A man and woman got out as he rushed
forward, frantically asking them to fetch help for the
unfortunate woman. Then, like the Good Samaritan, he stayed
to comfort her until others arrived.

Apart from his contact with the dead woman he had touched
nothing.

No one knew the Underwoods' version of events, but there was
nothing to suggest the lad was not telling the truth. His
shocked condition was a typical reaction to a traumatic
discovery.

'Just go through it all again, Stuart. You never know, you
may remember something which slipped your mind the first
time.'

He didn't. Asked to leave his blood-stained clothing for
examination he modestly turned his back on the detectives as
he removed his trousers and changed into clean clothes before
being allowed to go home.

Peter Acland didn't hurry his first task; too much rested on
him doing a proper job. Not only did his colleague want to know
every detail which may assist the enquiries; he also had to
protect his own professional standards for future accounta-
bility in the witness box while under scrutiny by defence
counsel, jury and high court judge. There are no half-measures
and, once begun, the task must be completed. Cole needed his
information now, but murder autopsies routinely take hours.

He had kept a lot of people hanging around by the time he
reached the car park. He knew the body would still be there,
which was important as it would give him a chance to evaluate
it against the scene of the crime. This first analysis often
helped him to piece together the picture and assess a sequence

of wounds and other events which would later be examined in greater detail.

He was greeted by familiar faces, old friends: senior detectives, Dr Norman Weston from the forensic science laboratory, the scientific assistants and photographers. Getting to grips with a job with this bunch was like pulling on a pair of well-worn, comfortable gloves. The pathologist was briefed in some detail.

'The body may have been moved slightly after the attack. She was found by a youth who gave her some comfort before she died and an ambulanceman may not have exactly replaced an arm after he tried to find a pulse. Otherwise she's where she was found, as you can see from the amount of blood. Her car's over there.'

Peter looked towards the red Vauxhall Astra; the driver's door still wide open, and he could see a handbag on the seat. From the car he traced the arc of blood spots to three large pools about five feet from the body.

Acland immediately saw enough to force one thought to the fore among many racing through his mind – psychopath! Blood marks contaminated the knees of the victim's trousers: she had crawled to her last resting place. This opinion was confirmed by blood deposits on the toes of her trainers, while the soles and heels remained clean.

Having assimilated the general scene it was time to get on with his task. The examination of the car park could safely be left in the hands of Norman Weston and his assistants. Wherever there was blood Norman was the best man to have around. Buckets of the stuff or microscopic traces made little difference; the meticulous scientist could usually work wonders with grouping techniques and distribution at a murder scene or with the clothing of victim or suspect. The cheerful Lancastrian, real-ale enthusiast and sporting buff, was a delight to work with.

It would be gratuitous to detail the misery inflicted on Carol Martin, and Acland's conclusions are all that are necessary: death from haemorrhage due to multiple penetrating wounds. As usual he was able to give other pointers to the investigation. A number of defence wounds on the hands and arms indicated a spirited attempt to ward off the knife. The preponderance of wounds to the left side probably meant that the assailant was right-handed, while the directional thrust of those in the back indicated a continuation of the attack as she tried to crawl away or lay helpless on the floor.

He was asked the inevitable supplementary question; detectives always had at least one up their sleeve. Usually it was to establish time of death, but that was already known.

'I suppose whoever did this is going to be covered in blood?'

Again Acland was at his magnificently frustrating best.

'Not necessarily. I should think it likely but I've seen cases where there have been horrible stab wounds and blood all over the place and the assailant has got away with hardly a speck on him. It doesn't necessarily follow that severe knife wounds are always associated with large blood loss but you've got enough at that scene to stand a chance of there being some on him – or her.

'If you don't believe me ask the surgeons at Birmingham Accident Hospital. They see the phenomenon more than I do and they keep the majority of patients alive – I only see the dead ones!'

Another question: 'Are we looking for a psychopath?'

'Possibly, but not necessarily. We don't know what caused it. People can fly off the handle without being psychopathic.'

Carol Martin's death had a dramatic effect on the commercial life of the town. Car parks became almost deserted and shopping malls sparsely patronized. The local police commander began receiving deputations of people wanting to know what efforts were being made to clear the matter up.

Plastered throughout the town were posters showing a recent photograph of the victim. They sought information from anyone who may have seen her or her assailant. Teams of detectives and police officers began retracing her movements and finding witnesses.

The usually introverted Stuart Hopkins suddenly became flavour of the month with his inquisitive classmates, who were anxious to glean details of the event occupying the attention of the town as well as the spotlight of the national media. Hopkins was different from other students: always conventionally and smartly dressed he rejected the casual appearance preferred by his contemporaries. He generally spurned close relationships and had no interest in female companions. Now, in the heat of publicity, he seemed to blossom.

'It's not every day you find a dead body on a car park,' he told a group of ardent listeners. 'The photograph on the posters is a good likeness of the lady I saw. I don't think the police have got enough evidence to prosecute a murderer.'

He underestimated a more mature and experienced mind when his witness statement came under scrutiny. Were his actions in the car park those reasonably expected of a nineteen-year-old lad, or for that matter someone of more advanced years, faced with such a devastating sight? Wouldn't the normal reaction be to panic and run the few feet to the stairway where help would be readily to hand, rather than undertake a drive around eight levels of a car park to the exit booths?

There was an additional factor. The basic tenet of homicide investigation, drummed into all embryo detectives at training establishments, is to be satisfied with the innocence of the person who discovers a body before looking further. Hopkins had satisfied his original inquisitors but now seeds of doubt began to materialize, although there was no evidence to contradict his story.

An opportunity to have a closer look at the youth soon presented itself. The press corps wanted to interview him; this would conveniently keep the case in the public arena, helping in the quest for further witnesses. He was invited back to the police station to see if he would agree; detectives also needed his fingerprints for elimination purposes. They had found a finger impression, albeit not a very good one, on the knife blade.

The short meeting with Hopkins was an unusual affair. He was accompanied by his mother and was diplomatically asked about the press conference. Cole sat in a corner of the room quietly assessing the lad. The proposal received immediate and determined opposition from Lorna Hopkins. Stuart appeared unconcerned at the prospect but was not allowed to speak for himself. Although the requests were directed at her son she consistently answered for him. Stuart just gazed through thick, heavy-rimmed spectacles towards the floor.

Eventually the entreaties were successful, but the mother insisted on being by her son's side. Throughout the conference she kept clutching his hand and telling him to breathe deeply to steady his nerves. Stuart sat impassively, apparently not finding the experience the ordeal his mother did. She told reporters:

'In a way I wish he hadn't found her and had to go through all this. But I'm very proud of him. I'm not surprised he did it. He was always a marvellous child.'

A recording of the event convinced those who watched that there was something very strange about this young man. They now had another priority: trace the couple who saw him on level 8 so that their stories could be compared.

The ploy to keep the murder in the headlines worked; lunchtime television carried pictures of Stuart staring blankly around the arena of reporters, lights and cameras, and it was repeated throughout the day. He was depicted as a hero.

The exposure soon produced dividends.

A young mother watching the lunchtime news dropped her cup of tea on the floor. Hopkins's face filled the screen. Within seconds her mother answered her telephone call:

'I know what you're going to say. I'm watching it as well. It is him – now you're not to worry – I'm going to ring the police and then I'll come over.'

Four years earlier the girl and her sister had been pestered by a youth who exposed himself as they walked home from school. After three occurrences the mother had had enough of his antics and informed the police. The girls described their tormentor as smartly dressed in school uniform and particularly noticed his bright red socks and thick-rimmed spectacles. One of them said she would never forget his sly, evil, horrible face and, indeed, the recollection made her drop her cup of tea.

Hopkins was suspected but denied everything. During an identification parade, the girls entered the room and, though he was no longer smartly dressed or wearing spectacles, this did not deter either of them from stepping smartly forward and pointing a finger towards him.

Later, at a juvenile court, Hopkins maintained his innocence and his mother told the bench that her son had never owned a pair of red socks. He was acquitted and his name never appeared on a police record.

In the early afternoon following the television broadcast a young detective opened the office door: 'A local woman's rung in, Gaffer. She reckons Hopkins is a flasher.'

News of possible developments spreads like wildfire through an incident room, creating an atmosphere of increasing urgency. An excited telephonist waved a sheet of paper. 'You may like to have a look at this message straightaway.'

The note read, 'That kid on the telly at dinnertime. He's a regular customer of mine – spends a fiver a time on porno mags and videos. He's a right weirdo – my assistant won't stay in the shop on her own when he comes in.'

The seeds of suspicion had germinated. Hopkins's vehicle was now subjected to close examination. A fragment of body tissue was found on the driver's door and traces of human blood showed up on the steering wheel, foot pedals and seat; so much for his story that he only managed to open the door before he heard an approaching vehicle. His soft-porn magazines were hidden beneath the carpet in the boot.

A small group stood around a table covered with polythene bags containing Hopkins's clothing. It was the shoes which attracted attention; the uppers were caked in blood and the soles and heels were clean.

'How the bloody hell did that amount of blood get there as he knelt by the body? He must have been standing underneath a torrent of the stuff.'

Norman Weston was too old a hand to start offering opinions before making a thorough examination in controlled laboratory conditions – particularly when he could see the evidence only through a polythene bag. He expressed mild interest but offered no encouragement. It was something else which attracted his attention: 'Hello – what's this?'

He pointed to a small tear below the left knee of the trousers; the clean edges were surrounded by blood stains. 'That looks like an incised cut. I'll have a look as soon as I get back to the Lab.'

When pieces begin to slot into place the jigsaw of an investigation often knits together rapidly. Sometimes it requires a little stimulation. An obscure finger impression had been found on the broken knife blade but contained insufficient detail for a straightforward comparison and was sent to the Home Office Research Establishment for enhancement. There is little point in making an arrest on a wing and a prayer when conclusive evidence may be available – particularly when a suspect has given a plausible explanation for his actions. Cole

made a telephone call to the local fingerprint bureau:
'I know it takes days; it always takes bloody days; but this time
it's going to take until tomorrow.'

Tina and Graham Underwood responded to press appeals and
another piece of the jigsaw slotted into place. They had been
stunned into inactivity for a few seconds when they saw Carol,
and then a young man emerged from the shadows, walked
slowly forward and bent over the body – actions hardly
consistent with a panic-stricken youth bent upon a mission of
mercy. He didn't utter a word. Then they volunteered to go for
assistance.

It was becoming more apparent by the hour that Hopkins
had some additional questions to answer, but they would have
to wait a little longer. The restrictions placed upon police
interrogation and periods of detention compel detectives to find
evidence rather than arrest on the basis of suspicion. But their
patience was soon rewarded.

Norman Weston was as good as his word. 'The amount and
distribution of blood on those shoes indicates the wearer was in
direct contact with a severely haemorrhaging body rather than
stepping or kneeling in a pool of blood.'

Other clothing told a better story, of patterns of blood stains
not easily seen during the cursory examination of the previous
evening. In the sterile, well-illuminated laboratory Norman
was in his element.

'Blood distribution on the lower half of the shirt's right
sleeve is consistent with a right-handed person striking
downwards at a blood-stained object. It certainly doesn't fit the
story of someone lifting a body covered in blood.

'The trousers are the most interesting. We haven't finished
the tests yet but the tear is an incised cut made by a sharp
instrument and would fit the width of the blade found in the
gutter. We can't say for certain until we have it back from the
fingerprint boys.

'I can tell you there's blood on the inside of the trouser leg
and it's not Carol Martin's. We haven't got a blood sample from
Hopkins but it looks highly likely he cut himself, because an
identical sample of blood is on a tissue in the trouser pocket.

'The last thing about the trousers: the blood distribution is
all wrong for somebody who says he knelt by the body. The
heavier staining is on the right leg below the knee – most of it

on the back, and it dropped there when the cloth was crumpled. I don't see how that could happen when the body is supposed to have been on the floor beneath the level of the trousers.

'How's that for starters?'

Although it would take weeks to ratify and corroborate the tests it was a good enough start; a fingerprint identification would put the icing on the cake.

Cole was in his office when he heard the news and walked the short distance to the fingerprint bureau. An expert was examining a photographed finger impression from the knife blade through a magnifying glass, comparing it with Hopkins's marks which lay alongside. In front of him was an enlargement on which he was marking identical features as he found them. The blade in its protective plastic sheath lay nearby.

'It's a left thumb, Gaffer, and it belongs to Hopkins, but I haven't found enough points yet to prove it.'

United Kingdom law requires the strictest level of proof in the world before a fingerprint can be accepted as undeniable evidence of identification. An expert can predict an identity after finding half a dozen similarities, but is obliged to establish sixteen identical characteristics before his opinion is accepted by a court.

'Give me another hour – I've only had it to work on for a few minutes. But there is something else which may be important...'

Don Folkes had worked with fingerprints for more than thirty years and knew his subject inside out. 'That mark on the knife was made by a blood-stained thumb, not a clean digit being pressed on a blade already contaminated with the stuff.'

It was a minor point which would later assume significance.

Cole kept the pressure on by staying in Folkes's office. His presence was not particularly appreciated by the 55-year-old fitness fanatic as clouds of acrid smoke began belching from the familiar pipe. It did the trick and within minutes the sixteen points were in the bag. There could hardly be greater suspicion that Hopkins was the murderer; but there were surprises in store and it would not be plain sailing.

Hopkins was arrested at Redditch College. 'Stuart Hopkins, you are being arrested on suspicion of the murder of Mrs Carol Martin. You are not obliged to say anything unless you wish to do so but anything you say may be given in evidence.'

He was closely watched for reaction but showed only studied unconcern.

'I didn't kill her. Can I get my coat?' No panic, fear, or other emotion.

The cut below his left knee was there for everyone to see as he was strip-searched in the detention room.

The space of four days had given him time to think of explanations but he offered none. Later, there came an unsolicited reaction. There was something he hadn't mentioned when making his witness statement. When he knelt beside Carol Martin he felt a sharp pain in his left knee and saw a knife blade; the handle was on the floor a few feet away. In a moment of panic he thought he would be blamed if someone came along, so he picked up the pieces and threw them over the edge of the building.

Forensic examination of material was at an early stage; enough had been done to seek answers to many questions but the shutters were up. Hopkins exercised his right of silence and refused to say anything more until he appeared in the witness box. He had given his explanation; detectives would have to get on with disproving it.

When Hopkins was taken to the police station on the Monday afternoon he was examined by a police surgeon to ensure he was fit to make a statement. Now he was examined again; this time the purpose was different.

The doctor probed the small cut. The internal direction of the wound was downwards towards the foot. 'Can you demonstrate how you knelt down, young man?'

A police photographer stood nearby, camera poised.

No matter how he tried the youth could not get the wound anywhere near the floor; it was well below the point of the knee. The knife blade would have had to be supported at least 45 degrees towards the vertical to cause the injury. It was impossible to visualize how a broken blade could have been supported in such a position on a flat concrete floor. Peter Acland later assessed the evidence and reached the same view.

One of the unfortunate consequences of homicide investigation is the effect on those nearest an accused. It is not unnatural that this sometimes manifests itself in a dislike of the policemen directly involved in a case, when lives are completely shattered by their necessary activity. Intrusions on privacy are inevitable at a time when relatives are in shock and unable to absorb the magnitude of what is happening. Detectives, while understanding these attitudes, never find it easy to come to terms with them; but lengthy experience eases the burden.

Stuart Hopkins was from an impeccable family whose parents lavished every advantage on him. There was no possibility they would accept the dreadful prospect that the child they loved could bear responsibility for murder. Their admirable support for Stuart never wavered.

It was under such a cloud of grief and disbelief that the family endured the detailed search of their home for anything which could link Stuart to the crime. They were forced to stand by as their son's immaculate and obsessively tidy bedroom was desecrated and possessions were listed, labelled and removed. Their apparent contempt for those involved in the investigation is understandable and did not detract from their inherent decency, nor did it diminish the amount of sympathy extended to them.

Those unversed in the criminal justice system would have reason to believe that the investigators had abundant evidence to convict Stuart Hopkins. But the detectives were practised in the system and knew the explanation he offered might be enough for a skilled barrister to influence a jury in his favour. Dissection is not the exclusive prerogative of the pathologist; it is conducted by lawyers on their briefs, and detectives on their cases. They must prepare carefully and leave nothing to chance. A jury must be convinced that an accused man has committed the crime for which he stands charged. Dissection, evaluation and analysis are the specialities of the homicide investigator. The easiest part of a case is often the identification of the person responsible for a crime; the hardest, to prove to a court's satisfaction that he actually did it.

When Hopkins was charged with the murder of Carol Martin, the task to convict him had only just begun.

The evidence was assessed. It needed further exploration and refinement. Norman Weston would no doubt have more to tell when his examinations were complete, but Hopkins's movements throughout the Monday would have to be examined in detail.

If possible one major problem had to be overcome. Witnesses

heard screams but no one had seen Hopkins before the Underwoods came along. Was there any way that he could have been
situated in the car park at the vital time? The inquiry team
collected car park tickets and till receipts, many with printed
times of transactions; there was also a starting time for their
deliberations. Marion Thomas was on a shopping expedition
with a friend and heard screams coming from the car park as she
looked at her wristwatch – it said 3.16 p.m.

Marina Pugh wound down her window at the ticket barrier. 'I
could hear screaming. It was high-pitched and seemed to be
coming from the car park but it only lasted momentarily. It was
very loud but I didn't realize what I had heard was the distress
call of a victim.'

These precise recollections seemed to offer an opportunity to
compare several witnesses' accounts with the one Hopkins had
given of his movements on level 8. A survey of all known
movements was carried out, but it needed a professional
scientific analysis to give it credibility in a court of law. The
departmental head of Industrial Ergonomics at Birmingham
University held the key. Three post-graduates studying for
Master's degrees were seconded to the murder squad and
worked alongside detectives on a series of carefully timed and
measured reconstructions using witnesses and documentary
evidence.

Every distance between fixed points was carefully analysed
and recorded before the young scientists, stop-watches in hand,
required witnesses to re-enact movements and indicate precise
locations where they saw or heard relevant detail. To establish
an average time each experiment was repeated three times. The
results were extraordinary: only three or four seconds separated
individual timings.

The unique opportunity for post-graduate research to assist a
murder investigation was justified by the production of a simple
multiple-activity chart. It illustrated in graphic detail that
Carol Martin's screams echoed around the car park between
three-fifteen and fifty-five seconds and three-sixteen and forty-
seven. It also showed that the Underwoods entered level 9 from
the shops as her screams stopped and they then saw Hopkins at
three-seventeen and thirty seconds.

Peter Acland estimated that the attack would not have lasted
longer than thirty seconds, given its frenzied nature, and time
had to be added for the disposal of the knife and a walk back to
Hopkins's car. All this was carefully reconstructed and the

conclusion was irresistible that he had actually been on level 8 at the time Carol Martin was killed.

Ergonomics was not the only scientific discipline employed in the increasingly complex investigation to discount Hopkins's story. Theories of movement and mass were employed to explain the manner in which the knife had been discarded. A series of experiments saw the knife hurled by a similarly built man from varying distances between the body and the edge of the building; each time they fell into the void between the buildings.

To project the handle fifteen feet vertically on to the adjacent roof it was necessary for the thrower to climb a metal guardrail and lean over the edge of a concrete wall to avoid the overhanging floor above. This was hardly the action of a panic-stricken nineteen-year-old; rather the deed of a deviant, discovered at the scene of a crime, unable to escape, but with a few minutes' grace to dispose of evidence.

More mundane evidence from fellow students gave the lie to Hopkins's account of his movements between the end of morning classes and his presence in the car park. They spoke of his reactions in the days before his arrest. He said the published photograph of his victim was a good likeness of the woman he comforted, yet a detective who knew her had not recognized her when he went to the car park. To another he described the stab wounds he had seen and the terrible injuries – originally he told police officers he thought she had been hit by a car.

Hopkins appeared before Mr Justice Tucker in the ancient oak-panelled Hereford Crown Court. The trial was a gruesome, sombre affair which touched the lives of its many participants. The jury received an early warning about the photographs, which had been reduced to the absolute minimum compatible with illustrating the ferocity of the attack.

'Examine the pictures as dispassionately as you can. You simply must face it.'

It was of little avail with one unfortunate female who fainted and held up proceedings while she received attention. Later she found it too much to continue listening to the litany of horror and was discharged. Hopkins's fate lay in the continued resilience of eleven of his fellow citizens. He was able to listen to everything with a mixture of studied indifference and occasional interest.

The case for the Crown was presented by Anthony Palmer

QC, an advocate admired for his preparedness and persistence. Detectives liked working with him because they knew he would have the minutiae at his fingertips. He did not rely solely on his brief, but regularly familiarized himself with the progress of events and visited locations relevant to a crime.

He outlined the case: 'Twenty or thirty seconds of mindless butchery ... boiled over from a frustrated mind of pent-up emotions ... a motiveless death ... no suggestion of rape or robbery ... Hopkins's ability to act coolly and persistently showed complete lack of emotion ... these are the hallmarks of a psychopathic killer.'

Yet he had to tell the jury the accused was of previous good character – he had never been convicted by a court and any mention of his previous alleged peccadilloes would have been seriously prejudicial to the defence case and is not allowed in English law.

Anthony Arlidge QC defended and objected to the description of his client as a psychopath; there was no evidence before the court to that effect, he said. ' ... the sight physically shocked the Defendant and took the colour from his cheeks – you can't do that by magic ... people act differently under stress.'

But the jury was getting the message.

A security guard told how he had recoiled in horror when he saw the injuries. He knew there was nothing he could do and he couldn't bring himself to touch her. Hopkins could do so, and mentioned the fact that she was wearing a wedding ring; the guard couldn't see any relevance in the remark. The lad was calmly telling her not to go to sleep as the guard stood rooted to the spot in horror; unable to do anything.

His mate, a first aider with a box of equipment, didn't bother to open it. He had attended victims before. 'Her injuries were horrible ... too bad for me to be able to do anything ... I was powerless ... I couldn't touch her.'

The first policeman to reach her was more used to gore but not in those circumstances; it was usually road traffic victims. 'She was still alive and I asked her who'd done this to her. Her lips moved and I bent down to try and hear but no sound came. She died shortly after. Hopkins was standing close by and told me he'd found her. He wanted to go but my inspector came and told him he would have to stay. He began to feel unwell and I sat him in my police vehicle while the ambulancemen gave him oxygen. He later left with a detective and the police surgeon.'

Dr Jim Phillips told the court of his original concern for the young man. He made sure he was well enough to make a witness statement. Hopkins showed signs of shock and he gave him a mild sedative. He made no mention of an injury to his leg. Four days later he examined the cut and asked Hopkins to demonstrate how it had been caused. In his opinion the explanation didn't hold water.

Peter Acland's unpleasant task was to describe the injuries and give his opinion as to how they had been inflicted. Twenty-one wounds on the back, when the victim had been on her knees or prostrate on the floor. One wound dissected the voice box – no wonder she had been unable to speak. Wounds on the hands and arms revealed a spirited defence against the knife before she had fallen to her knees.

Norman Weston entered the witness box with a dossier inches thick to describe his findings. An audible gasp ran through the court as he donned Hopkins's blood-spattered shirt to demonstrate how the blood distribution was caused by repeated downwards thrusts with the right arm. He was equally convincing in explaining the direction of flowing blood which contaminated the shoes and trousers. Smears of blood on tissues from Hopkins's pockets showed that he had wiped blood from his leg wound as well as Carol's blood from his hands. Her blonde hairs, found on the inside of both trouser legs, gave the undeniable impression that they were already on Hopkins's hands when he tended his wound. Then a chilling piece of evidence. He had not found blood on the soles of Carol's trainers and could only conclude that she had been on the floor for most of the attack.

A demonstration of his impartiality was the fact that he examined the car park, lifts and stairways for other traces of blood. He found some in the lift and on the stairways. They were not of Carol Martin's or Hopkins's groups; but he did not find that unusual. In his experience it would be unusual if one did not find some evidence of blood in a busy town centre.

Tina Underwood faced a hushed court as she explained how she and her husband came across the murder scene. They had been stationary for about four seconds when they saw the youth emerge from the shadows.

'He didn't walk quickly towards the body ... he touched her face ... he never said a word.'

Detective Superintendent Derek Knight had wanted Hopkins's assistance to keep the matter alive in the media.

Two days after the killing he was still anxious to secure more witnesses. He had no evidence to suspect the youth but had begun to feel uneasy about the young man when he read over his statement. The experienced officer's intuition led to Hopkins's undoing.

'It just seemed unusual that a lad of nineteen would behave in that way because Mrs Martin was really quite a horrifying and distressing sight after the attack. A much more natural reaction would have been to run down the stairs, shouting for help. It seemed to me that he had reacted in a way that I never would have done at his age, and even today.'

There were some diversions explored by the defence: a blood-stained youth seen in nearby toilets during the fatal afternoon had been traced. He'd been scrapping and his opponent was also found. A woman with a cut hand came forward after press appeals with a satisfactory and innocuous explanation.

Another youth who was seen leaping over the retaining ground floor wall of the car park at about four o'clock had not been traced. He had a stain on his jeans but who was to say it was blood? In any event, police officers had been swarming all over the building for a good half-hour by that time. The vagueness of the information and the time differential did not deter the defence from presenting the unknown youth as the phantom killer.

Hopkins described his actions to the jury exactly as he had told the police and resisted a vigorous cross-examination from Anthony Palmer. He was an unusual spectacle of calm indifference. He admitted a life of social isolation; he didn't mix well or enjoy the company of girls; he didn't drink and spent a lot of time alone. His mother was the person closest to him and he described her as his best friend. He told her he had knelt on the knife when he arrived home on the Monday afternoon and she put a plaster on the cut. If he had told the police about the injury or the knife they wouldn't have believed him!

It took the jury six hours of deliberation to convict him of murder – an indication that they gave a great deal of thought to balancing his explanation with the weight of evidence the prosecution advanced against him.

In stentorian tones, Mr Justice Tucker told him: 'I cannot recommend a minimum sentence in your case as you are under twenty years of age, but this was a ferocious and sustained attack on an innocent lady. The sentence is fixed by law:

custody for life.'

Carol Martin's husband watched the young man descend the dock steps. Keith Martiin had been sitting within feet of him throughout the trial; he felt the need to do so in support of his wife and to try to understand something about her last few hours. Having seen justice done he paid a moving tribute to her memory and spoke of a deep feeling, based upon his belief in God, that somehow good would come from the tragedy.

Hopkins's parents watched in disbelief as their son was led away. Lorna, who was clutching a Bible, collapsed in tears, screaming 'Oh, Stuart'. The couple had been present every day and at each adjournment visited the cathedral in silent prayer.

The lives of two ordinary, inherently decent, families had been destroyed by thirty seconds of mindless violence.

For the second time within a year David Cole watched a young man, attracted by pornography, sentenced for murdering an innocent housewife going about her normal affairs. How he wished some of those who refused to recognize the effect of such material on young minds could have witnessed what he had seen.

No one will ever know why Carol Martin was attacked. Did Hopkins expose himself to her or make some indecent remark? If so, she would have been expected to react.

A bald sequence of events is all that can be deducted from the combination of scientific analysis and eye-witness accounts. Carol returned to the car, unlocked the driver's door and placed her handbag on the seat and shopping in the rear. Then, attacked with the knife, she ran towards the centre aisle before being felled and mutilated. During the frenzy one of the blows missed its mark and found her assailant's leg; as further blows rained down her blood splashed his clothing. Hopkins ran to his car to escape but was thwarted by the Underwoods' approach. Having to account later for the blood on his hands, he walked to his victim and touched her face. Given a few minutes' grace he had disposed of vital evidence but could not consider leaving without heaping further suspicion on himself. He decided to play the Good Samaritan and face things out.

There wasn't a hope in hell he would get away with it.

4   Dabbling with the Devil?

The Philip Booth Case

Charlie Miller was out cold. It had been a heavy night and a late finish. The frantic hammering on the front door gradually penetrated his fuddled brain, and he began to come to sluggishly on hearing someone shouting through the letterbox.

'Chas, wake up, wake up! It's Phil – he's been hurt.'

Charlie suddenly realized that he wasn't dreaming and woke with a start as he recognized the voice of Andy Newell who lived with Phil Booth a couple of blocks away. Charlie had been on the booze with them; it seemed only minutes before. His head pounded; he had no idea of the time, but it was still dark.

Pulling on his jeans and shirt he hobbled towards the door.

'Hang on, I've got to find my boots.'

He found a light which worked; most of the fittings were without bulbs. Charlie who was in his early twenties, lived alone and was not particularly houseproud. Eventually he got something on his feet and grabbed a coat. Opening his door he found Andrew Newell leaning against the wall. By the cringe he looked rough!

Not that Andrew was ever particularly well dressed. He usually wore the same clothes: jeans, leather jacket and calf-length Doctor Marten boots. His long, lank hair completed a picture of dishevelment, and this morning his deathly white features and sunken eyes did nothing to enhance his appearance.

As Charlie opened the door Andy took off down the concrete steps towards the entrance and, still befuddled, he struggled to keep up, hardly noticing that daylight was breaking as they covered the seventy-odd yards. They raced up the steps to the door of the first-floor flat and the mists of alcohol and sleep cleared in a flash as Charlie looked into the hallway. There was blood everywhere; congealed pools of it covered the floor, swirls and splashes decorated the walls. He did not notice at the time that all the marks around the walls were no more than eighteen inches off the floor.

Andy was standing in the hall looking towards the lounge and Charlie joined him. He saw a bundle of blankets on the floor and a pair of feet sticking out. Bending over the bundle he unwrapped the body of young Phil Booth; he was stark naked and had been swaddled in the blankets like a baby. Charlie saw cuts in his chest but no sign of blood coming from them. The boy was deathly pale and his whole body was smeared in blood. As he looked, horror-stricken, he distinctly saw the injured boy's chest heave and heard a long sigh.

'Bloody hell, he's still alive. Go and ring for an ambulance – quick.'

Charlie now felt completely helpless; he didn't know what to do. He replaced the covers and stood up. He picked up a leather jacket lying behind the door and dropped it quickly on to a chair as he saw it was soaked in blood. He suddenly needed fresh air and went outside.

Constable Millington found the two young men at the foot of the communal stairs. He had been patrolling the slumbering and amorphous housing estate on the southern edge of Telford when he received the call from his control. He was much closer than the ambulance and could have saved them a journey. When he looked down on the pathetic bundle of blankets he could see that Philip Booth was dead.

Charlie Miller followed the policeman into the flat but Newell stayed outside.

Millington turned round. 'What's been going on here then, cocker?'

'It's no good asking me – I don't live here. Andy Newell knocked me up a few minutes ago. He and Phil lived here – you'd better ask him.'

'Well, go and get him, please.'

There was no chance of that. Nineteen-year-old Andy Newell refused to go inside when Charlie told him his mate was dead. He whispered, 'I suppose I'd better tell them the truth.'

But Millington was only able to report to his control: 'A youth lying naked on the floor – blood everywhere – looks as if he's been stabbed in the chest. His mate says he's been out all night and came back about six o'clock and found him. No signs of a forced entry. Can you get me some assistance and a doctor to certify death?'

The duty inspector arrived with the police surgeon and spoke to Newell. 'When did you last see him?'

'About two o'clock. We went back to the bonfire to collect the empty bottles and when he stopped to roll a fag I sat down by a wall and went to sleep. A bloke coming past on a motorbike woke me up and I came back here and found him and all the blood.'

There were a few garbled details about a party and an argument earlier in the evening but the inspector couldn't make much sense out of it. He told Millington to take the two young men to the police station while he sorted matters out at the scene.

'How long's he been dead, Doc?'

It was a confusing picture. The pools of blood on the hall floor were congealed and darkening in colour, and the splashes on the walls were dry. A glance in the bathroom revealed much more on the wall and around the lavatory pan. It had all been deposited some hours before and yet the body gave all the indications of recent death.

The police surgeon, a well-known and popular GP, immediately appreciated that the time of death might prove crucial. The body was still warm to the touch; the limbs had only just begun to stiffen with rigor mortis and the blood, still within the circulation, was only now beginning to settle under the pull of gravity. The boy had not been dead very long. A rectal temperature, measuring the heat from the core of the body, confirmed the impression. It hadn't dropped very far below the normal thirty-seven degrees centigrade. That was always supposing his temperature had been normal to start with. He might have been ill, feverish, hypothermic or overheated from muscle exertion. The room was cold, the body naked and he had probably been drinking alcohol. There were so many factors which the good doctor knew could send his calculations way off target. This wasn't a uniform metallic sphere in the controlled conditions of a physics laboratory. This was a human, *was* a human, and even in death they provided surprises – as Acland would later find out.

The doctor looked at his thermometer. 'I think he died between six-thirty and seven o'clock.'

The inspector looked at his watch. It was just after

seven-thirty. 'He's obviously died a violent death. Call the detective chief superintendent and a Home Office pathologist.'

The telephone call came just after eight o'clock. A senior detective 'on call' over weekend periods is never surprised to be contacted; statistically it is a time when most violence occurs. Many happy social occasions end in argument and violence; a few in tragedy.

David Cole was put in the picture by a detective.

'Newell says he came home and found him close to death just after six this morning. He went to a mate's house for help and they called an ambulance. The police surgeon confirms the time of death at about six-thirty but there's a lot of blood around and the state of it indicates an attack some time earlier. There's no sign of any forcible entry to the flat and there's no obvious weapon lying around the body. I've called Peter Acland and the forensic people out.'

Cole arrived at the flat an hour later and cautiously made his way across duckboards laid across the hallway towards the lounge. He viewed the blanketed body and the disturbed furniture, then looked briefly at the bathroom. There was a lot of work to do but he decided to wait for Acland to arrive before going further.

A few minutes later he was leaning against a gate leading into the garden of an adjoining ground floor flat when a door opened behind him. Bert Williamson, a wizened little man in his mid seventies, had the misfortune to live in the flat directly beneath the two young men. He was used to a certain amount of a noise but the previous night had been exceptional and he was unable to sleep. His curiosity was aroused when he saw the bulky figure in a dark overcoat leaning on his gatepost.

'What's going on – is something up?'

Cole turned around and passed the time of day.

'Did you hear anything from the flat upstairs during the night, guv'nor?'

It was just the trigger necessary to get the excitable little man going. 'Hear anything? Hear anything? I'll say I heard something. A bloody racket – went on all night. Like a lot of bloody banshees stamping around.'

Then as an afterthought: 'Why – who the bloody hell are you?'

With the introductions completed, Cole calmed him down and listened to his diatribe about the previous night.

Bert had gone to bed at about eleven thirty and was woken some time later by noise from the flat above. He guessed it was between one and two in the morning. A number of people were stamping about, dancing in unison. It went on and on so the old man moved into a chair in his living-room. There was no escape and he spent an interminable time listening to the incessant din. He probably dropped off for a time until a door crashed shut and woke him again. He thought it was about five o'clock.

His story, interspersed with opinions about the younger generation, did not lead Cole to anticipate a sympathetic reaction when he told him there had been an 'incident' and one of his neighbours was badly injured. Bert simply turned on his heels, muttering expletives about noisy, selfish bastards and slammed his front door.

Cole briefed Peter Acland as they sheltered from the cold, damp November wind behind a nearby fence. 'There's something iffy about the time of death, Pete. Blood congealing all over the place and from what I've been told all the activity was around two o'clock. But he's supposed to have been alive at six-thirty when his mate found him and that's confirmed by the doc.'

Acland groaned inwardly. Whenever he worked with this man he always seemed to have an obsession about the time of death.

They entered the flat, carefully treading the line of protective duckboards placed across the floor. They were joined by the ubiquitous photographer and a scientist. Blood-staining was heavy along the hall floor and its lower walls, particularly near the doorway to the lounge. Adjacent to the front door was a bathroom where crumpled and blood-stained jeans, underpants and socks lay on the floor in front of the basin. There were blood smears on the toilet seat, basin, floor and adjacent wall.

On the living-room floor Booth's naked body lay in front of a settee, almost on his back but slightly inclined to the right. Two blankets, one orange and one grey-white, were beneath the body but also covered the legs and lower trunk. A blood-stained towel was near the head which was resting on a cushion seat from the settee. At the feet lay a blood-soaked T-shirt and on a nearby armchair a leather jacket and a cut-away canvas jacket, similarly stained. A spatter of blood traversed a wall mirror.

Acland knelt carefully beside the body. Much of its front had been wiped and faint traces of dried blood were smeared over the chest, abdomen, pelvis and legs. He saw immediately the likely cause of death. Four closely grouped penetrating wounds on the chest, exactly over the heart. That much appeared obvious. He was cautious not to jump to conclusions, but there didn't seem to be any other injury severe enough to have caused death, although his definitive opinion would have to await his comprehensive examination in the post-mortem room.

It is always important to see a body *in situ.* Corpses are difficult to handle and move. Understandably they must be confined and hidden from view while transported. Vital clues can be lost, despite there being measures to preserve them.

Acland noted that the soles of Booth's feet were blood-stained; he had walked barefoot in blood. This could be important. As the picture was only just beginning to be put together no one knew which particular detail would be important or otherwise. The blood on the feet could have been accidentally wiped off by movement, or it might later be claimed that it could have been transferred while someone manipulated the body, moving blood-stained hands from one part to another during the autopsy.

Ridged characteristics, similar to a fingerprint, were found in blood on the side of the left thigh. Much time was spent figuring out the best way to preserve this potentially vital evidence, but after a delay of several hours and many phone calls it seemed that photography, after all, was the only effective method. In the event, the clue led nowhere. It wasn't necessarily a fingerprint but could have been part of a hand or foot impression, as those areas of the body bear identical characteristics.

At the mortuary Acland was able to explore the injuries in detail. The wounds to the chest were closely grouped, very closely grouped. Three of them penetrated the chest and converged at the apex of the heart. The accuracy was impressive. They could not have been caused haphazardly during a prolonged fight. They were inflicted when the victim was immobile or unsuspecting. One of the wounds had not penetrated as deeply as the other three, but all were orientated in the same oblique way. The largest measured no more than a centimetre and a half in length and its initial appearance implied that the blade of the knife might have been double-edged. Later, when the edges of the wound had dried, the appearance of a notch at one end of the wounds suggested a single-edged blade. He might have been wrong; some knives are double-edged along part of the blade and single-edged towards the hilt.

Acland found some more injuries: a bruise on the right forearm; a V-shaped split in the scalp at the back of the head; an abrasion above the right eyebrow; and the suggestion of a faint bruise to the lips. A long but not particularly deep cut on the back of the left wrist indicated that a blade had been drawn over the wrist – perhaps as the victim moved his hand to try and push away the plunging knife.

A body doesn't bruise after death but often faint bruises, not noticeable at first examination, develop to become visible some time after death. With this in mind Acland took a further look at the body a few days later. He noted additional bruising on the left elbow and over the knuckle of the left hand. More significantly he discovered groups of small round bruises on the top of both thighs. These suggested to him that someone had been pressing down with their fingertips on that area of skin. Was it restraint? Was there more than one assailant, or could it be the victim himself clasping and squeezing his own thighs in the agony of his condition?

One remaining question troubled the pathologist: the blood on the soles of the feet. Given his severe injuries, could the victim have moved around the flat? The wound to the back of the head could have been caused by a blow from a blunt instrument, but was more likely caused by falling backwards heavily against a hard corner of furniture. The ruptured scalp would have bled externally much more readily than the chest wounds; but how long could he have survived with the three severe wounds to his heart?

Cole was somewhat surprised when Acland said it would have been possible for the lad to stagger around for a short while before collapsing to the floor, even long enough to go to the toilet, undress and return to the living-room. But when he collapsed, death would have ensued quickly, in minutes rather than hours. He very much doubted that the chest wounds could have been inflicted in the early hours and the victim still be just about alive at 6.30 a.m. This time, however, there would be a surprise for Acland.

Like many new-town developments the Brookside estate at Telford is a study of contrasts in everything but the uniformity of its design and buildings. A perimeter road encloses its inhabitants within a web of culs-de-sac and enclosures served by a central complex of shops, pub and community centre. It is populated by predominantly decent, law-abiding families who keep themselves very much to themselves, but whose tranquillity is constantly interrupted by an element of irresponsible youngsters and petty criminals. Philip Booth and Andrew Newell were prime examples of a shiftless minority always at odds with authority.

Philip had moved with his family to Telford from Cheshire. He found employment as a farm worker and proved himself an industrious lad. In 1986 his mother and father left the district and their twenty year old son moved into a flat with his friend, Andrew.

In many ways they were an unlikely pair. Philip had experienced minor scrapes with the police and was a heavy drinker; he was also not terribly bright. Andrew was a twin from a large family. He had a good academic record, and his abilities were no doubt encouraged by highly intelligent parents and stimulated by the achievements of his siblings at university. For some inexplicable reason he dropped out midway through A levels and left home. After a brief spell living with an older brother he joined Philip at Brookside and found a job as a forestry worker.

The bond between the two youths seems to have been a shared fondness for general scruffiness and outlandish behaviour. They dressed similarly and associated with a group of 'bikers' – the term is used here to describe their mode of dress rather than the vehicles they rode. Not one of the group owned a motorcycle, although such transportation dominated their conversation.

The 'bikers' met at the Lakeside Tavern where they were regarded more as a liability than as favoured customers. On Saturday 8 November 1986 they planned a bonfire in isolated woodland on the outskirts of Telford alongside a large industrial estate. Although it was close to Guy Fawkes's Night, the anniversary seemed to have little to do with their particular celebration. At closing time they made their unsteady way towards Halesfield Woods after a night of heavy drinking.

Philip Booth had already drunk eight pints of beer and earlier in the evening persuaded Andrew to give him thirty or forty 'magic mushrooms' collected during work in the woods. To everyone's astonishment Philip ate the lot and then emptied a two-litre bottle of home-brewed beer.

Magic mushrooms are not difficult to find in the countryside.

They contain the hallucinogenic drug psilocybin, and in common with most crude drugs obtained from natural sources the 'dose' in any given species varies depending on its stage of development, growing conditions and genetics. The susceptibility of the abuser is also variable. But one thing is for sure: a mixture of large quantities of alcohol and an equally substantial amount of magic mushrooms is certainly going to have a confusing and bewildering effect on the brain. It may manifest itself in excitement or stupor, confusion, anger or tranquillity, and even a mixture of all those emotions, as the abuser passes from one phase to another. The only predictable thing about psilocybin is its unpredictability.

A few hangers-on joined the party, and joints of cannabis and beer started to circulate. There were no fireworks, at least not of the pyrotechnic variety, just a huge bonfire constructed from vandalized trees. The jollifications went on into the early hours, the isolation of the venue creating no nuisance to anyone.

In various degrees of drunkenness the group broke up; Philip and Andrew were among the last to leave. It was almost two miles back to the flat and after two in the morning before they said goodnight to their remaining companions.

Bert Williamson was not the only person disturbed by noises. A neighbour on the same floor was in bed watching a video when he heard loud voices and some banging about. It did not last all that long. A couple walking a dog around the flats some time after two o'clock heard raised voices and heavy footsteps running up and down the stairs. Once the noise subsided the estate slumbered on until people woke to a dull, cold Sunday morning.

Shortly after six o'clock a seventeen-year-old lad made his way to work on the Halesfield estate. His route was along the footpath used by the 'bikers' a few hours before. Through an underpass beneath a dual carriageway he saw, in the headlight of his scooter, a large bundle of rags on the floor. As he passed he saw the 'rags' were in fact the prostrate body of a young man in dark clothing, fast asleep, with his face turned towards the wall. The noise of the machine in the confined space disturbed Newell and, shaking himself back to consciousness, he made his way back to the flat where the injured Philip Booth lay in the final throes of death.

* * *

It did not take long to trace other members of the group on the Sunday morning. They all told the same story about the party. Philip Booth was drunk and Newell was well on the way.

An examination of the flat showed that Philip Booth lost a great deal of blood. His movements round the rooms and corridor could be tracked by following the splashes. Most haemorrhaging had occurred in the lounge, but at some stage he went along the hallway to the bathroom. He crawled on hands and knees, brushing walls and doors as he passed. In the bathroom he slumped on the toilet and leaned against the adjacent wall. On the floor near to the sink lay his blood-stained jeans, underpants and socks. It appeared that he had taken a towel back to the lounge to staunch the blood flowing from his chest, before wrapping himself in blankets and lying on the floor to die. The saturated carpet beneath the body was evidence that life's blood had slowly drained away.

The other rooms appeared uncontaminated by blood. The only bedroom was used as a store and contained nothing but junk. Andrew Newell used the tiny boxroom; his single bed and chest of drawers effectively filled it. Philip Booth always slept on the settee in the lounge. The kitchen was a muddle of dirty crockery and scraps of food.

The links of heavy metal chain, which hung from a clothes' hook near the front door, matched marks embedded into walls, ceilings and doors in the lounge and along the passageway. The chain had obviously been swung with considerable force, and blood spots around one of the marks indicated that at least one of the blows had found its mark.

Cole opened the door to Newell's room and got his biggest surprise. The walls and ceiling were covered with sinister-looking posters and graffiti. At the head of the bed was the drawing of a sheathed dagger, and a length of chain lay on the floor. A ceremonial dagger adorned the window-sill. There were no signs of disturbance nor blood and he closed the door. Within the boxroom lay an object which would later prove of surprising significance to the inquiry. It would also put the posters, dagger and chain in a clearer perspective.

The majority of detectives are sceptics, who take nothing at face value. The two young men had been invited to recount their version of events. Charlie Miller's was substantially the same as the one he had already told Millington. There was nothing to place doubt on it and he was eventually released.

Newell stretched credibility to the limit. He and Philip Booth had drunk too much during the Saturday evening, but Philip was in the worst state. It was therefore a little surprising that after staggering two miles home they decided to return to the bonfire to collect some empty beer bottles. Another walk of four miles! When they reached the wood it was so dark that they could not see anything and began to walk home. At the entrance of the underpass Philip paused to roll a cigarette. Andrew sat on the ground and fell asleep. Then the scooter roared past and he ran back to find his friend lying in a pool of blood.

Cole didn't believe a word of it. 'Lock him up. You can interview him properly when we've got a better picture of what happened inside that flat and heard what the other "bikers" have to say for themselves.'

Newell had never been in trouble with the police before. His reply when told he was being detained on suspicion of murder was a little surprising for someone described as an innocuous youth.

'I suppose you're going to twist and fix everything up, but you won't get me ... I've done nothing.'

Some hours later, when the cell officer paid him a visit, his confidence had melted. He was close to tears. 'He went mad. He was swinging a chain round. I had my knife. It was the only way to stop him. I just kept plunging it into him.'

The startled officer immediately summoned a detective to listen to his story.

The drunken pair had argued over a couple of pork chops Newell had bought for Sunday lunch. Booth wanted to eat them there and then. He became aggressive, took a length of chain hanging in the hall and chased Newell into his bedroom, wrenching the door off one of its hinges to get at the cowering youth who bolted back into the lounge as the chain fell across his back. In the mêlée Booth picked up a knife and came towards him, smashing the chain against walls and ceiling. Newell knocked him down and Booth hit his head on the corner of a cupboard. Momentarily stunned he dropped the knife and Newell took the opportunity to seize it.

'I stabbed him, I don't know how many times. I just don't know how it happened. He stumbled back and fell on the floor. I panicked, grabbed my overcoat, put my knife in my pocket and went out'.

After panicking, and running from the flat, he made his way towards his parents' home. He stuck the knife in a crevice of a stone wall and ran in the opposite direction towards Halesfield Woods. He lay down in the underpass and went to sleep until woken by the scooter. When he returned to the flat there was blood everywhere and Philip Booth was still alive, though convulsing and breathing shallowly. He ran to Charlie Miller's for help.

The case seemed straightforward now, particularly when he took detectives to recover the knife. On the way he asked a favour. 'In my bedroom there's a record case. There are things in there which are private. I can't say what they are, but will you promise me not to open it?'

By that time Cole had gone home. After a thirty-six-hour stint he deserved a rest. The job was well wrapped up. When he returned the following morning he would only have to tidy up the odds and ends before leaving the paperwork to the divisional boys. His optimism was short-lived.

Cole was not alone in thinking it was an uncomplicated matter which would eventually revolve around legal arguments as to whether Newell was guilty of murder or manslaughter. A solicitor told magistrates at the first remand hearing that Newell conceded his friend's death was his responsibility. He was overcome with grief and worry. The solicitor had no objection to the press reporting the circumstances from the outset; he thought it important for everyone who knew the quiet, nervous and unaggressive young man to be told how the killing came about.

Newell had been remanded to prison when Cole arrived back at the incident room. On his desk lay a maroon, plastic-covered record case enclosed in a polythene bag. A detective relayed the conversation with Newell.

'Well, what's inside it?'

'We haven't opened it. We thought it had better wait for you. It wasn't because he asked us not to Gaffer.'

'I should bloody well hope not,' Cole growled.

'It's because we think it might be important. We found it in his bedroom on top of a chest of drawers. It was right next to a couple of pork chops – the ones they'd been fighting about.

We've found some blood on both sides and on the bottom, so we'll have to be careful with it.'

Cole put on a pair of protective gloves and gingerly took the case out of the polythene sheeting. Several detectives crowded round. Newell's mysterious request made it seem now as though Cole were turning the key of Pandora's box.

As he raised the lid a detective policewoman gasped: 'You know what we've got here, Gaffer, don't you?'

He had a fair idea.

A few years previously a team of his detectives spent months investigating a child sexual abuse case involving satanic rituals. It led to lengthy terms of imprisonment for those involved and received national publicity. The detective policewoman had researched the occult and knew about the ceremonial artefacts of witchcraft, satanism and black magic. She was now looking directly at some.

Carefully the contents were placed on the table. It was a significant discovery and took hours to analyse. Fourteen books about the supernatural, alchemy, time travel, mythology, witchcraft, chaos magic, and marked catalogues from specialist dealers, indicated a deep interest. But the bits and pieces in the box would for certain give the lie to later attempts to minimize Newell's interest in evil.

A piece of thick graph paper had verses written on it.

> Torches blaze. And secret chants are praised,
> As they start to cry, Hands held to the sky,
> *In the night, The fires burning bright,*
> The ritual has begun. Satan's work is done,
> 666, the number of the beast,
> *Sacrifice is going on tonight*
> I'm coming back. I will return,
> I will possess your body, and I will make you burn,
> I have the fire, I have the force,
> I have the power to make my evil take its course.

Four words written beneath the verse had sinister connotations: Satan, Leviathan, Lucifer, Belial – all synonyms of the devil. The sign of the anti-Christ, an inverted crucifix in human blood, had been smeared on the bottom.

Candles, cloths, Tarot cards and a bone-handled dagger complete the paraphernalia. Was the dagger the 'Athena', a symbol of the greater powers of evil?

Unfortunately for those who tried to minimize Newell's

commitment to the occult he had committed some of his experiences to paper. Two notebooks described his mystical experiences in graphic form. He was able to make things happen by exercising mental powers. On one occasion he was sitting in front of a mirror when his face turned into a werewolf; then the image of his head disappeared and he could see the wall behind him. He described occult skills and the power he claimed over everyday objects. He could concentrate attention on electric lights and other appliances and switch them on and off at will. He made people and animals passing by the flat stop, turn and look towards him.

> ... I had a strange feeling of power. I felt a force flowing through me. It made me feel good and fit and strong in mind and body ... I soon discovered that I could make things happen at will by thinking about it.

Some time later he was lying in bed reading *The Grimoire of Chaos Magik*.

> I felt all powerful. I prayed to Baphomet to help me in any way possible and in return I offered him my services and asked him to appear to me in my dreams or in real life.

Were these innocent experimentations, the ramblings of a sick mind or the sincere thoughts of someone committed to evil forces? Conclusions could not yet be drawn. What Newell had to say would be important and he would soon be given the opportunity.

When Cole briefed his team they began to put two and two together. One young detective sent to photograph the underpass where Newell had fallen asleep looked through his proofs. He remembered graffiti on the concrete walls and examination confirmed his suspicions.

'There's a lot of Satanic symbolism there, Gaffer – drawings of the Devil and other figures.'

They visited the underpass; it was a draughty place to fall asleep on a cold November night. A mass of symbolism covered the wall – Satanic, obscene, racist and stupid.

Cole stood in the doorway of Newell's room. The walls, covered in graffiti about warlocks, witches and mysticism, now assumed some significance. The drawing of the dagger was identical to the one he had found in the box. One of the door hinges was broken, but there was not a speck of blood to be seen inside the room.

Scientists were still working on the flat – it took ten days to complete the task – and Herbie Perriton spent a couple of hours describing their deductions. Droplets of blood that fall vertically on to a hard surface form star shapes on impact, while drops projected horizontally through the air force their volume weight forward when they hit a surface and form pear shapes. From these directional shapes it is possible to plot the position of different parties to a fight, and the path of a weapon used to inflict the injuries. Similarly, an injured person walking or crawling will drip blood on to the floor and brush against walls, leaving a story of his or her passage.

The flat was beginning to divulge its secrets. Philip Booth had a rare blood group possessed by only one in every two thousand people. All the blood around the flat belonged to him, including the smears on the record case. The mass haemorrhage occurred in the lounge, but at some stage he had struggled to the bathroom to remove his clothing. The record case had been placed on a wet patch of blood before being returned to Newell's room by someone with Philip's blood on their hands. It could not have been carried there by the victim because there was no trace of blood within the room.

Cole carefully made his way through the flat. All the advice and information he received made the apparent simplicity of the crime seem increasingly hard to believe. After an initial reluctance to admit the truth Andrew Newell made a frank confession. Then he made the strange request about his record case, which, along with the graffiti in the underpass and bedroom, complicated matters. Medical opinion was that Philip Booth died soon after the knife wounds had been inflicted, but the row took place at about two o'clock and he was still alive at about six-thirty. The injured youth had struggled to the bathroom, but conflicting advice suggested that the severity of the wounds would render such movement impossible.

Peter Acland put another spanner in the works when he examined the knife Newell had hidden in the wall. It was just too wide. The maximum width was 2 centimetres yet the wounds in the victim's chest were only 1.5 centimetres wide at most. Human skin may stretch marginally under pressure and knife wounds are usually slightly larger than the width of the blade. These were 25 per cent smaller. Dissecting and measuring the passage of the wounds through the tissues to the heart, Acland concluded that the probable shape of the

weapon was thinner and more gently tapering than the one
with which he was comparing them.

A forensic scientist came to the same opinion. He dismantled
the knife but, unusually, found no trace of blood. He then made
test penetrations with the knife into the clothing worn by the
deceased, and the incisions were similarly wider than the
wounds. Either he and Acland were both wrong or there was
some other reason why Newell had led detectives to the wrong
knife.

There were so many imponderables. With Philip dead, only
Newell could give the full story; others could offer only
opinions. Cole turned to his medical friends for help.

Eventually Peter Acland was able to ease his mind about the
time of death. Sections of heart muscle from the area
surrounding the knife wounds were studied under a
microscope. The edges were heavily infiltrated with minute
blue dots. The pathologist at once recognized them as acute
inflammatory cells, the body's early response to injury. The
cells migrate from the bloodstream to a damaged area to fight
possible infection. They begin to move into position almost
immediately, but the numbers he saw must have taken several
hours to reach the wounds and he also knew that the cells do
not move very far after death. Cole's information about the
timing of the disturbance against the time of death now
seemed realistic. Acland knew from experience that some
victims with wounds to the heart survive for a short time, but
they were usually those with single wounds entering just one
chamber. Here there were three holes transfixing almost the
full width of the heart.

Now sure from his microscopic examination that Booth had
survived several hours after the wounds to his heart, the
pathologist was somewhat surprised. He took Cole to the world
famous Birmingham Accident Hospital to meet his friend and
colleague Keith Porter, an accident surgeon with considerable
experience in the treatment of knife wounds, who, with his
colleagues, had prevented many a victim passing into Acland's
hands. Unfortunately in the large urban area of Birmingham
the occurrence of accidental and malicious knife wounds can
amount to several in any given week.

Porter was surprised by the story and diagnosis, but not
entirely perplexed. He had known many patients walk into

hospital with wounds to the heart. Much depended on the position of the hole in the heart wall, as natural contraction of the muscle can form a partial seal and the sac surrounding the heart can create a tight compressive compartment. In other cases it can have the opposite effect and allow blood to escape freely. There were always many variables in the human condition, but certainly this case was to prove one for the record books.

The predominant feature of the case, which amazed the workaholic surgeon as he studied the photographs, was the accuracy of the four wounds. Localized grouping and convergence towards the apex of the heart – that had taken some precision. Even an experienced surgeon must take care to locate the exact area on the chest before making an incision to reach the apex of the heart a few inches below. His opinion – that these wounds had not occurred in a face-to-face confrontation at arm's length – had to be respected. It appeared to be an attack of surgical accuracy; the heart had been penetrated, not once or twice, but three and almost four times. Perhaps the one incomplete thrust had been thwarted by the victim being jolted into activity by three unsuspected but rapid thrusts, this also accounting for the cut on the wrist.

Newell's friends, shocked by Philip's death, remembered events which had made them uneasy, and his workmates on the forestry estate recalled conversations which they had then taken for youthful romancing. Stories of irrational behaviour emerged. He had an interest in the occult and did not hesitate to converse about it. They laughed at him when he said he would put a spell on Charlie Miller, but began to think more seriously when he told them that he slept in a churchyard tomb.

They remembered Philip Booth telling them that after a heavy drinking session he had woken up in the middle of the night. Newell was standing in the lounge holding a knife, then ran from the flat screaming, 'I'm going to kill somebody.' They all referred to the incident later in Newell's presence but he shrugged it off.

On another occasion Newell threatened two youths with a beer glass and pulled a knife. One of them knocked the weapon from his hand and kicked it across the floor. Newell raged about the treatment of his knife rather than the fact that he had been disarmed.

In the weeks before Philip's death Newell spoke of headaches and blackouts which he attributed to a fight or from eating magic mushrooms. Indeed, on the face of it he appeared a confused young man who drank far more than was good for him and supplemented his alcohol consumption with dangerous substances.

Cole tried to establish the significance of the record box. He wanted to know if there was an important relationship between the symbolism in the underpass and that in Newell's room. He spoke to historians, academics and authors about the forces of evil and clandestine practices. They knew about the historical perspectives of witchcraft but little of its practices.

There was agreement that the Saturday night had the ingredients for the practice of devil-worship: fire, darkness, a gathering at midnight; knives, chains and the impedimenta of an altar. Excessive consumption of alcohol and hallucinogens would have released the inhibitions of participants. The quickest way to attempt to resolve the mystery was to confront Newell with the facts. He had every right, however, to maintain the privilege of silence.

Cole sat opposite Newell. A solicitor was present to protect the young man's interests and he had been told of the second thoughts the experts were having about the knife. The defence had accepted the coroner's offer of a second post-mortem and their expert pathologist had the same misgivings as Acland. His views had obviously been communicated to Newell.

Reassured by scientific opinion he faced his questioner with some confidence as he sought to retract his confession. He still admitted that when he and Philip fought they were the only two people in the flat and he did have a knife in his hand – it was the knife he had shown the police. He couldn't remember exactly what happened but he probably struck out before he ran out of the flat in a panic. But he knew he couldn't have stabbed his friend because 'the forensics' said it wasn't his knife.

The young man leaned back in his chair. Cole could read his mind – the expression on his face said it all: Get out of that.

But the detective hadn't finished, and a textbook interrogation followed. Producing the record case from beneath the desk he saw a hardening of Newell's expression.

Were the two keys in his pockets the only ones which would open the box? Did Philip Booth have any access to the contents?

No one else had a key and Booth didn't know anything about it.

How long had it been in the bedroom? When was the last time it had been taken out?

He had taken it into the lounge about a month before the fight and when he had finished with it had put it back on top of the chest in the bedroom.

Did Booth enter his room on the night of the fight?

He only got as far as the door.

Only one person in two thousand had Philip's rare blood group, which, in real terms, meant only sixty people in Telford's 120,000-strong population. The marks on the case were that type of blood. How did he account for that?

He couldn't – he hadn't moved it out of the room that night and he didn't know who had. He had difficulty dealing with this persistent question and mumbled indistinctly.

Cole turned to the contents of the box.

What about the notebooks and the descriptions of his power surges?

Just imaginative writing. He had an interest in the occult but never practised it.

Why the dagger?

He just liked knives.

Were the pieces of material altar cloths?

No, just old rags.

The candles had been used – wicks were scorched. If they were ceremonial candles it would mean he had indulged in occult practices.

That was daft – they were only ornaments.

So the box itself was not an altar.

No, it certainly was not!

Everything, apart from a mild interest in the supernatural, was denied.

Cole had, however, left his *pièce de resistance* until last. From a drawer he pulled out the sheet of graph paper. There was a distinct swallow and a nerve started to throb at the side of Newell's neck as he clenched and unclenched his jaw.

It was only a few verses from a song. He had the LP – it was in the flat.

Cole knew all about that. But why had he found it necessary to write four synonyms of the devil underneath the verse?

No explanation was forthcoming.

The cross at the bottom of the sheet. What did it mean?

Just a cross.

But it's an upside-down cross – you know what that means, don't you?

No reply.

That cross was made in human blood. Whose blood was it?

It was probably his.

Cole couldn't argue. It had not been possible to classify the sample. What explanation was there for the piece of paper and its content?

A shrug of the shoulders and no reply.

Why the sign of the anti-Christ?

No reply. The young man was beginning to realize that the police had been thorough in their enquiries.

He told people that he slept in a tomb in Stirchley churchyard!

Only once when he had come home too late to disturb his parents.

Couldn't he see anything unusual about that as a place to sleep?

Not really – it had been for a bit of a dare.

He was getting rattled now and began to contradict himself.

He may have collapsed in the underpass when he returned to the bonfire.

A few minutes later:

He was sure he had fallen asleep. There was no question but that he had collapsed.

He didn't know anything about the graffiti on the wall above his resting place. It certainly was not somewhere that he regarded as a sanctuary.

He then started to deny things said during his previous interview:

He had never seen blood gushing from Philip Booth.

He got the idea into his head that he stabbed his mate, that's why he said he'd done it. But now he knew it wasn't him because the knife didn't fit.

Relentlessly the interview continued.

Why tell three different stories?

The first was a cover-up. The second was what he thought the truth was. The third was what he now knew the truth to be.

Newell could not disguise his evasiveness.

With a new account of the fight and Newell's denial of

responsibility for Booth's death Cole waited for the results of forensic tests with added interest.

Newell had blood marks on his jeans when he was arrested, but from previous experience the detective knew that the distribution of blood can play tricks and lead to misinterpretation.

A chest wound, even one penetrating the heart, may not bleed much externally. Most of the blood can be trapped inside, around the heart, either in the sac itself or spilling into an adjacent cavity. A T-shirt might soak up what external blood is lost and there is no spray or gush as the knife is removed. Most of the blood, smeared and paddled around the flat, probably came from Booth's head wound or his wrist. The spray of blood across the mirror could have been flicked there as he removed his T-shirt. It was conceivable that the person who stabbed Booth could well have very little or no blood upon him. His contamination would be further minimized if he left the flat before the blood had been spread around. He may have been unable to avoid only one or two spots. This wasn't a case where a head wound had been repeatedly hammered in which case each blow causes blood, welling from the previous injury, to splash up.

Booth's death was one of these unusual cases. He lost most of his blood and his movement around the flat ensured its widespread distribution. Charlie Miller had managed to avoid most of it. He went into the lounge and leaned across his injured friend before picking up his blood-stained jacket. It was the area where most blood had been deposited, yet he rushed out of the flat with only a trace of blood on the soles of his shoes.

Andrew Newell had no blood on his shoes, but his jeans bore traces classified as belonging to Booth. His only action had been to push open the door of the lounge before panicking and fleeing when he saw his friend staring lifelessly into space. The traces were all below the knee. A long overcoat which friends said he was wearing at the bonfire party was never found and though the ashes of the bonfire were carefully sifted nothing was revealed.

It was the experts' rejection of the secreted knife as the murder weapon which caused Cole most concern, but as enquiries progressed he became reassured.

Newell had an obsession with knives. A pocket knife was found in a jacket hanging in the hallway and it corresponded with the dimensions of the wounds and cuts in clothing to the satisfaction of Peter Acland and other forensic scientists.

Why did Andrew Newell conceal a knife which was not likely to be the murder weapon? An explanation, which he would always deny, is that a knife used in satanic rituals assumes supreme significance for the practitioner. There is a duty to protect it from harm so that its powers for evil are not affected. It was a suggestion which some treated with incredulity.

Newell's legal advisers faced the situation with equanimity and no little urbanity. They had offered his confession at the preliminary court hearing and could not reverse their decision to lift the ban on reporting subsequent court proceedings. As a consequence the public were treated to titillating tales of witchcraft and satanism in their newspapers.

Two months after the killing Newell's solicitor told the magistrates he now denied the offence.

'At the time he was first seen admissions were made to the police that he had murdered the sad and unfortunate Philip Booth by the use of a knife, and a knife was provided to the police as the murder weapon ...

'It's not that he was not telling the truth, he was telling things as he had seen them at the time.'

'He [Newell] just wanted the court to know, and his family wanted the court to know, that he did not murder the unfortunate deceased....'

Another month went by before ritualistic behaviour was mentioned in court. Newell was fighting hard to be released on bail and the prosecutor threw in the bombshell as he sought to justify a further remand in custody.

'You may feel there was some sort of "ritual sacrifice" element to the killing.'

The defence solicitor was quickly on his feet:

'The nearest this case gets to black magic would be if I brought out a box of chocolates. Evidence of magic, werewolves and ritual sacrifice are fanciful explanations for the mystery of Booth's death.'

The prosecutor was undeterred. 'Newell had claimed that the stabbing was self-defence, Booth had gone mad and attacked him with a chain. But then he told the police not to open his record case ... the opinion of an expert was that it was a black magic altar ... it contained the impedimenta of witchcraft ... the central implement in any sacrificial act would be a dagger.

'Notebooks ... purported to give results of experiments Newell carried out in psychic power.

'It would appear he had many thoughts of causing death. He had discussed the possibility of ambushing and killing someone almost at random walking through the town park. His friend, the deceased, had told his mates about being woken in the night by Newell holding a knife declaring that he was going to kill someone!'

The evidence of sleeping in the tomb, strange graffiti in the bedroom and underpass were all publicly aired at this early stage.

The defence solicitor struggled to minimize the force of the prosecutor's assertions:

'How many werewolves are seen running about in Telford?'

'The suggestion is ... unbelievable. They are looking for solutions to their mystery ... If Newell had stabbed Booth he would have been covered in blood. After three days of police questioning he began to believe he had killed his friend and made the admissions.'

What the last statement chose to ignore was that Newell had confessed to a police officer completely unconnected with the case within a day of being taken into custody.

The bail application did not succeed and Newell remained in custody for months before his trial. There were a number of sceptics who tried to dissuade the prosecution from placing any emphasis on the notion that Philip's death was connected with anything more sinister than a drunken altercation.

Timothy Barnes QC, the prosecutor, had no doubt as to what was the most effective course of action.

'What happened after the two men went into the flat is known only to the defendant and the dead man.

'It is quite clear that between 2 and 3 a.m. Mr Booth sustained the fatal injuries.

'In Newell's bedroom the police found a box stained with Booth's blood. It must have been in contact with Booth's wet blood before it was taken back into the bedroom ... the contents of the box included a number of pieces of material which showed he was quite clearly familiar with black magic practices.

'It was moved by Newell after he struck the fatal blows, having taken it, for reasons which may be a matter of speculation, into the living-room, where the wounds were inflicted.

'I must inevitably suggest that this killing may have had, in Newell's mind, some black magic or occult significance. That suggestion I do not make lightly.'

For the next two weeks witnesses gave testimony on the various aspects of the case. The tedium of doctors, scientists and detectives sifting the minutiae of the crime was relieved by discussions of evil doings.

A historian gave evidence that the sign of an inverted cross suggested a rejection of Christ and that inscriptions found on the walls of Newell's bedroom could mean that he was interested in black magic.

A writer describing herself as a ceremonial magician thought that the contents of Newell's record case were associated more with white magic, which she explained was beneficial and healing. Black magic, by contrast, was deliberately cruel and harmful.

Timothy Barnes read from a book: '... the use of a table or altar for use in magic ceremonies. A small box which contains all your magical gear can be used as an altar if necessary. The box should be kept under lock and key as its power can become dissipated if things are left about.'

She agreed that Newell's box seemed to fulfil those recommendations but only once did she place a sinister connotation on Newell's impedimenta. 'The inverted cross in human blood at the end of the Devil poem is not a sign of modern magic. It is a very old practice.'

Acland conceded many propositions put to him by the defence barrister. Yes, the wound to the back of the head might just have been caused by Booth catching his own head as he swung the chain around; and yes, the finger-pressure bruises to the thighs might have been caused by a third person restraining the victim. But he was adamant that the fatal wounds were no accident. They were not the wild lunges of a man trying to defend himself. He disagreed with the scientist who had earlier given evidence that in his opinion Booth had been helped to the bathroom. Acland thought the youth could have made it on his own. Perhaps he staggered there on his feet and crawled back on all fours. That would account for the blood on his soles and the deposits on the lower reaches of the walls. He gave his views on the knife and the effect the head injury would have had on the victim's state of consciousness. The defence had picked up a few points to give the jury something to think about but had not managed to dent the main theme – that it was a deliberate killing.

Among the many blood marks on Philip's body was one on the left thigh which showed patterns similar to a fingerprint. Because it did not match the finger impressions taken by the police from Newell and Booth, the defence embarked enthusiastically on an attempt to convince the jury that someone other than Newell must have been involved. Their fingerprint expert measured his words carefully; he was very experienced and realized the consequences to his reputation of a dogmatic approach.

'So far as I can see from the forms available Andrew Newell did not make that impression.'

Did it belong to Philip Booth?

'So far as I can judge from the forms available it did not.'

He was as helpful as his professionalism would allow, and was careful to use the phrase 'the forms available'.

Don Folkes, a police expert, with over thirty years' experience in the examination of fingerprints, put matters in perspective.

'The mark on Booth's body may have been made with a foot, palm or side of the hand which all bear the same ridged patterns as fingerprints. The defence expert was only able to examine forms showing finger and palm impressions. It is impossible to record all ridge markings from other areas of the body. While it is therefore always possible to prove the positive with fingerprints it is very often impossible to prove the negative.'

It will never be known whether the suggestion of supernatural forces played any part in the jury's consideration. Within the confines of their room they may have ridiculed the whole thing. Newell's confession and his earlier remark to Charlie Miller ('I suppose I've got to tell them the truth.') may have had greater impact.

If they were influenced by his initial acceptance of guilt they may also not have been overly impressed by his subsequent attempts to evade responsibility.

Either issue did not take long to influence a decision. The eight men and four women took just over an hour to return a verdict of guilty.

Mr Justice Leggatt was brief and to the point: 'You have been found guilty of murder. The sentence of the court is fixed by law. It is life imprisonment.'

In July 1989 the case was back before the appeal court. Defence counsel, Martin Wilson QC, argued that he had been unable to raise the issues of self-defence or provocation at the trial because Newell maintained that he had not been in the flat when Booth was killed. But in one of the accounts Newell had given to the police he said the death had been in response to the chain wielded by his friend. It was now claimed that he was provoked into protecting himself and this possible explanation should have been put to the jury by Mr Justice Leggatt. The tribunal agreed and Newell's conviction was replaced by a sentence of seven years for manslaughter.

The 'magic box' was never mentioned. That particular mystery remains.

5 Aristocratic Angst

The Dale/Illingworth Case

The sunny mid-September Friday in 1987 was a time to savour. David Cole and Allen Mayo had little to tax them in the form of serious crime. They made the most of it by visiting detectives in the western outposts of the Force, a luxury on which they could not often afford to spend the time. The afternoon found them in Clun, a small village where there are no detectives but whose village pub serves a good lunch! Lying within the Welsh Marches it is remote from the centres of crime and Cole had never been there before.

As they made their way home through the Shropshire countryside Mayo broke the silence: 'Got anything on this weekend?'

'No, nothing special.'

'It's my weekend to take the calls and we've been invited to a drinks party on Sunday lunchtime. It'll be sure to go on a bit – would you mind taking them for the day?'

Cole agreed and went on to make one of the most unfortunate predictions of his career: 'There's one thing for certain, I won't be called out here. I can only remember one big job in the last twenty years.'

Mayo often reminds him about the conversation. It took place as they sped past a lane leading to the hamlet of Hopton Heath, where a blind eccentric called Simon Dale lived alone in a rambling mansion house. As they passed, this man had just set off on his last journey into the outside world, walking sightlessly along the lane to buy vegetables for his evening meal.

* * *

Sunday, 13 September was a pleasant enough day, but the chill evening made the prospect of a leisurely bath and a couple of drinks before bed an inviting prospect for the 'on call' detective. Cole's expectations were shattered by the shrill summons of the telephone.

'Why does it always have to be at the weekend?'

'Suspicious death at a place called Hopton Heath, near Bedstone, Herefordshire, sir. Detective Inspector Matthews is in attendance and has asked for you – Dr Acland has also been called. The body is at Heath House – an old man lying in a pool of blood in the kitchen. It looks as if he's been battered about the head. There's no sign of forced entry but there's been a fight. That's all we have. Can you give me your ETA?'

Cole needed reminding of the location – forty-five to fifty miles away – and worked out that he would require at least an hour and a half to get there. It was already getting dark and not the easiest cross-country route, but that was of little concern. He knew the local detective inspector would have everything arranged. He also knew that he would not be idle, for Derek Matthews had a very inquisitive nature.

The journey took longer than anticipated and it was well after ten when Cole found himself approaching Hopton Heath. Flashing blue lights indicated that he was at the right place and he drew alongside a police sergeant at the gateway to an imposing drive. An old friend, Ray Heighway, leaned through the car window.

'You'll remember this place, Gaffer. This is where Arthur Prime shot Dr Beach twenty years ago.'

Although he had only played a minor role in the earlier matter Cole was now the victim, not only of his unfortunate prediction, but also of a remarkable coincidence: it was the second murder to have occurred in exactly the same place within twenty years.

As anticipated, Derek Matthews had things well arranged. Cole walked towards a Jacobean mansion beneath huge trees swaying in the gusty breeze. He looked into a rear lobby, his route prescribed by the familiar duck-boards. Garden chairs lay on the floor and Matthews pointed to a bunch of keys beneath them. Blood splashes covered the walls and a door leading to the kitchen. He looked round the partially obstructed door and became immediately aware of the stench of putrefaction from the body of a large, elderly man. The corpse lay on its back causing the obstruction; a pool of congealed blood spread across the floor.

'Bloody hell, it's hot in there, Derek. Who is he? Do we know when he was last seen alive?'

Matthews had spent the last couple of hours anticipating the flood of questions. 'It's hot because the cooker's been on all the time. He's called Simon Dale. Apparently he's almost blind and lived alone. We've spoken to the lady who found the body – she called with some papers she's working on for him. He had readers supplied for him and she was one of them. His divorced wife lives across at Docklow but apparently she's always here painting the house and doing the garden with a couple of their kids. From what I've been told it's a funny set-up. She owns the place and wants to sell it. He just refuses to budge. There's been a lot of aggro; it's been going on for years.'

News spreads like wildfire in the countryside. While the two detectives waited for Peter Acland, snippets of gossip reached them from local people who were 'in the know'. Matthews was right: it was indeed a funny set-up.

Simon Dale was an obsessive and capricious character, who lived in fading gentility in the rapidly deteriorating Jacobean mansion. He had lived alone since his wife walked out in 1973, taking their five children with her, and survived all subsequent attempts to oust him from the family seat. His only company since then had been when one or other of his sons chose to stay for a few brief periods.

His middle-class background was perfectly conventional. The son of the Oxford Diocesan Architect, he qualified in the same profession and was later, in 1939, commissioned into the Royal Engineers. He enjoyed an unremarkable war and was invalided out in 1944. A hereditary eye defect had worsened to the point where he had been unable to hide it from the authorities. The continuing deterioration of his vision shaped the future pattern of his temperamental behaviour and character.

Dale was a large man, with a personality to match. He had an aloof and dismissive manner while his booming upper-crust accent guaranteed attention. In his younger days he was very much the man about town. Despite failing eyesight he drove an open-top Lagonda with great panache. No one remembers him doing much work, but there are plenty who recall his zest for life and exuberant love of parties, as well as the company of pretty girls. He mixed in company far beyond his means or social status and developed a taste for the high life. His forthright views on a variety of subjects invariably drew an audience of impressionable young females.

The whirlwind bachelor existence continued into his thirties. He knew his days as an architect were numbered and his financial situation worsened. The frenetic lifestyle had been aimed towards joining the ranks of the upper classes and he became increasingly frustrated at his failure to do so. It was therefore a chance too good to miss when he at last made his mark on a girl fourteen years his junior. She was the epitome of all he had been looking for: a good-looking true-blue aristocrat with a fortune. Within months they were married and the fateful relationship between Thomas Simon Savage Dale and Susan Cecilia Mary Wilberforce was consummated.

As Cole and Matthews waited outside the house they were joined by another colleague, Geoff Daniels, who had been checking the doors and windows.

'There's no sign of any forced entry, Gaffer. Keys on the floor behind the back door and blood up those walls make it look as if he opened the door to somebody. There's some valuable stuff inside but there's no obvious gaps where anything's been removed. The only significant thing I can see is a lot of shoe impressions all over the place. The wooden floors are as dusty as hell. They're mainly moulded soles or trainers. A lot of them are kids' sizes – it looks as if some youngsters have been running around.'

Peter Acland and Dr Norman Weston of the forensic science laboratory arrived, and while Acland's stay was brief Weston was destined to spend weeks with a team of scientific officers examining the house for clues. The immediate task was to survey the scene with Cole and try to reach a view about the circumstances leading to death. Dead men cannot speak but very often make excellent witnesses, providing a sequence of events as well as vital clues.

Shrouded in anti-contamination suits, the three men stood over Dale's body and looked around the room. A huge refectory-type table had been moved sideways. Splashes of blood lay along its surface and extended on to walls and other furniture. There was a smashed basin on the floor and a number of sherry glasses on a work surface, one of which was partly filled. Prepared vegetables were strewn across the table and an oven dish in the cooker contained a charred mass. When the body was found the shutters had been drawn and the light on. The victim had obviously been preparing an evening meal before he unlocked the door.

Questions began to race through the investigators' minds. Did the sherry glasses indicate that he had had visitors? If he lived a reclusive life, what were children's footprints doing all over the house? More importantly, when had he last been seen alive?

Acland's first concern was to be sure they were dealing with murder. Of course, it looked like murder. The old man was lying in a pool of blood – there were also spatters of it on the table – and signs of a disturbance in the lobby ... but the pathologist hesitated. He did not want to be responsible for dozens of police officers embarking on a wild goose chase, at a cost to the taxpayer of thousands of pounds a day, if it were all an accident. The narrow entrance hall was cluttered with household artefacts, many stored on high shelves; some were at arm's reach even for a tall man. Could he have been trying to reach something when it fell on him? Perhaps the deckchairs had been stored in a precarious fashion, only to fall whilst the poorly sighted man was rummaging around. Had he then staggered into the kitchen to collapse heavily against the table?

The blood on his head had dried and it wasn't possible to see the wounds clearly. They would need to be cleaned and studied at the mortuary. The body showed the early signs of decomposition: slight slippage of the skin; some production of gas; and a greenish hue to the skin. The neck showed an area of deeper discoloration – the blue-purple of almost certain bruising. Almost certain? Again Acland hesitated, knowing that putrefaction can play many tricks on a less-than-wary examiner.

'I'm pretty sure we've got a murder, but at this stage I'm not completely ruling out some freakish accident; we'll have to—'

The careful opinion stimulated an irritated response from Cole: 'What! With blood sprays on the bench, and on the far side of the table?'

'I know, I know. We'll assume it's a murder unless it proves otherwise later. I just don't want to jump to too many conclusions...'

'You bet we'll assume it's a bloody murder.'

Acland knew and dreaded the detective's next question.

'Well, how long has he been dead then?'

'Now you're asking something. The trouble is, it's been very hot in here. The cooker's been left on and the heat has accelerated decomposition. Taking the body temperature is going to be a waste of time ... I've seen cases where they can get into this state in twenty-four hours.'

'Yesterday then?' It was more of a statement than a question.

'No, not necessarily. It might have been as early as yesterday, but I couldn't rule out the day before. Certainly not today, and I doubt if it were much earlier than Friday.'

The body was 'taped' by the scenes of crime officer to secure possible clues which might still have been adhering. Then the pathologist moved forward for a closer look. Dale was lying on his back alongside the table, with his head near the hallway door. The arms were flexed on to his chest and he was lying on the electric lead of a dictating machine, which ran from a wall socket to the machine on the table. Acland continued his routine examination aloud.

'No obvious stab wounds, no signs of asphyxia – I'm pretty sure this is a bruise across his neck ... it's diffused now over the whole of the neck, but there seems to be a more prominent band of bruising extending from the left ear across the left and front of the neck. When you're ready I think we can move him.'

The pathologist had earlier had much the same difficulties as Cole in locating Heath House. He was even less enamoured when he later found there was some uncertainty about which coroner's area they were operating in. Depending on the jurisdiction, the body had to go either twenty miles north to Shrewsbury or twenty miles south to Hereford. Shrewsbury would have been marginally better for Acland. Once on the M54 he could get home easily, enabling him to snatch a couple of hours' sleep. He had court in the morning and no way could he get out of that. The body went to Hereford. Acland got home in time for breakfast.

Simon Dale, who had resisted all attempts to remove him from Heath House for many disputatious years, finally left in an undertaker's metal coffin. Before leaving for the mortuary Cole drew Matthews to one side.

'If he's divorced I suppose the next of kin must be his eldest child. Do we know how many of them live with the mother at Docklow? We'll have to inform someone because we need formal identification for the coroner. Take Dave Clark with you and see his ex-wife.'

The senior detective was uneasy.

'I shall be interested in the reaction you get, Derek. Don't let on too much and stick to the basics. Break it to her that he's dead and just say we are looking into the circumstances.

Matthews and Clark did not know the small village of Docklow, a strip of houses either side of a main road, twenty-seven miles from Heath House. They were looking for a residence whose size would fit the name they had been given: Forresters Hall. The only similar address a local could suggest was Forresters Hall Cottages, just down the road from the village pub. He knew that a rather posh lady lived there, but she never took part in village life.

It was well after midnight as Matthews approached the cottages. A number of newish vehicles in the driveway implied that the occupants were unlikely to be agricultural workers, for whom the houses were originally built. Walking towards the door he intuitively shone his torch inside the vehicles; behind the rear seat of a large Peugeot estate, light reflected off a slender metal object.

Clark knocked on the door. There was no reply. He then hammered on it and heard movements inside. No lights were switched on but after some minutes a pale young man opened the door. Marcus Wilberforce told the detectives that he had telephoned the local police station when they began knocking, because he thought they may be drunks. He invited them inside, but did not ask what they wanted. There was an awkward silence as they shuffled about in the hallway.

Matthews was deliberately uncommunicative until a slender, middle-aged lady appeared, fully dressed in a smart two-piece suit. Inviting them into the lounge, she gestured towards a chair and sat opposite the inspector. Baroness Susan de Stempel sat ramrod straight and composed, her hands folded neatly in her lap. She turned dark eyes towards him, her thin lips pursed in a straight line. He felt as if he had been granted an audience with a being vastly superior to himself.

Still no one asked why the officers were there in the dead of night. Matthews at last broke the silence. 'There's been a problem at Heath House.'

'Has he burnt it down?' Hardly stopping to draw breath she told them all about a long-standing dispute with her ex-husband over the property.

Although he was able to reassure her about the safety of the house neither she nor the young man asked for any other details. Eventually Sophia and Simon Wilberforce came into the room and Matthews told them all that Simon Dale had been found dead. The bombshell was greeted in complete silence and he was slightly unnerved by the absence of any reaction. Sophia was the first to speak:

'Was it inside, or out?'

This was followed by a query from the baroness: 'Has the place been broken into?'

That question was repeated several times throughout a stilted conversation. The two young men said very little; Marcus showed signs of unease, while Simon was indifferent.

Matthews identified the group as Dale's former wife and three of his children and established their movements over the weekend. He had to listen to details about the conflict over the occupation of Heath House and the atmosphere which had prevailed over previous months. The baroness was anxious to emphasize that she owned the property and that she resented Dale having visitors. She was particularly keen that Matthews should know he had had visitors the previous Friday evening and told him that she had taken the number of their vehicle.

Matthews prepared to leave. He glanced around the lounge and entrance hall at the beautiful antique furniture and artefacts which crammed every available space. As a detective working among rural gentry he had been in many fine homes, but had never seen anything like this. At the front door he paused.

'Could I have a look in the estate car, madam?'

Without question the baroness fetched her keys. Matthews bent inside and retrieved a metal poker from the floor behind the driver's seat.

'Are you taking that away with you?' When he said yes, she did not ask why.

Matthews summed up the encounter as the two men travelled towards Hereford to report to Cole.

'I've never met anyone like that in my life and I've never seen anyone, particularly kids, fail to show any reaction whatsoever when told of an unexpected death in the family.'

The chances of Matthews, or anyone else, meeting someone like Baroness Susan de Stempel are fairly remote. There are few like her about. Born into the aristocracy, a scion of the anti-slave campaigner William Wilberforce, she possessed a manner demanding deference. Although privileged by class and education she had what many would consider an unfortunate childhood. Her father, a professional soldier and squire of the Yorkshire village of Markington, was killed during the Second World War. His pre-war duties took him and his wife abroad for lengthy periods, and Susan and her elder brother, John, remained behind in the care of relatives and nannies. Later they were boarders at Catholic public schools and, in the fashion of the times, Susan was groomed to fulfil the role of society hostess rather than qualify academically. She had a rebellious nature which did not endear her to educational establishments, and her stance was perhaps an early indication of things to come.

Her mother, Cecilia Wilberforce, remarried shortly after the war, again into landed gentry, and their relationship became somewhat distant. The marriage terminated Cecilia's financial interest in the Markington estate and it was divided between the two children when they reached their majority. Meanwhile, an aunt accepted responsibility for Susan's 'coming-out' in the season of 1953. Lady Illingworth was well accustomed to such burdens. Her late husband's wealth had helped the Markington estate survive for several years and they accepted much of the responsibility for Susan and her brother throughout their childhood.

There was a serious disagreement when Susan reached the age of twenty-one and insisted on selling her share of the estate. It had been divided amicably, John keeping the Hall and a proportion of land while Susan had the remaining acres and a commercial quarry. Uncle Robert, a London solicitor and younger brother of her father, cautioned against a hasty sale, but the headstrong girl would have none of it. For the first time in her life she would be financially independent, able to pursue any lifestyle she desired.

In 1957 she met the flamboyant 37-year-old bachelor, Simon Dale. After a whilwind courtship they married, much to the disapproval of her family. When the first child was born, they decided that the stifling atmosphere of London was no place to bring up a family and began looking for a country property.

Susan was comfortably off, but Simon had been professionally shiftless. Till now, he had earned little money and his failing eyesight meant the prospects could only worsen. They were both possessed of grand ideas and Susan had fine furniture and paintings from her legacy, but nowhere to put them. Once again her headstrong nature came to the fore. They discovered the almost derelict Heath House on the Shropshire/Herefordshire border, within a few miles of the home of her mother and stepfather. It would have been demolished within days if, seemingly on impulse and with little thought about cost of renovation, they had not bought the property. It proved to be an albatross around their necks, which eventually led to unhappiness and penury.

Heath House has an imposing façade, which continues to impress travellers along the adjacent road. It conceals the ravages of time and the intermittent efforts taken to keep one step ahead of disaster. In the early years the roof was made weatherproof and several rooms renovated at the cost of a large part of Susan's wealth. More children came along and Simon still failed to secure commissions. By 1964 they had five children, a partially renovated house and an income of about twenty pounds a week from a family trust.

In any domestic conflict there are always two sides to the story, but it is beyond doubt that after the birth of the fifth child the relationship between the couple soured. There were claims of violence and perversion which are always difficult to substantiate, or deny. Simon, frustrated by the failure to realize his social and professional aspirations, withdrew into a world of rapidly declining eyesight and isolated himself from his family. He was at first obsessed by theories relating to causes of, and cures for, his hereditary affliction and later he became engrossed with the notion that his home featured in Arthurian history and legend.

While much emphasis was later placed on the obsessions, there is another side to Dale's character which did not achieve such prominence. He was a gregarious individual, fond of companionship and attention. His much younger wife belonged to a class content with their own company and she was a good mother to her young brood, deriving pleasure from their development. She had no need to be in regular contact with her relatives or to develop relationships in the community. Within the context of financial and domestic difficulty two such diverse personalities were bound to clash.

In 1973 they divorced and it was decreed that Heath House should be sold and Simon obliged to move out within two weeks of the exchange of contracts. No details of a settlement of the proceeds were established. Susan finally left in 1975, while the children were away at school, and thereafter she provided the youngsters with a home, although they maintained contact with their father to varying degrees.

Susan's departure set the stage for the saga of Heath House. Simon was determined to remain and over time became increasingly reclusive and obsessional. Susan, with fluctuating enthusiasm, tried to have him removed by legal means. Both existed on limited finances, the children being privately educated through the compassion and generosity of Susan's relatives.

A measure of the bitterness which developed between the couple is indicated by the fact that in the years following the divorce the children changed their surname to Wilberforce. It was an indication of Susan's reverence for her illustrious forebears. In this she was not alone; the reputation of the eighteenth-century emancipator is never far from conversation with any member of the family.

The early attempts to dispose of Heath House were always frustrated by Dale's conduct. He obstructed agents sent to value the premises and openly discouraged prospective purchasers. He extended his view of the Arthurian connection by claiming that the king's seat lay within the grounds and solicited support for a further idea that an ancient Armenian settlement was hidden within the cellars of the house. Such wild theories were used to support his continual tenure.

Meanwhile, his former wife lived in rented houses, or with relatives, while her main asset deteriorated amid a jungle of vegetation. She settled at Forresters Hall Cottages in 1977 and her financial situation eased as the children became more independent. As a result, she lost some of her earlier enthusiasm to dispossess Simon Dale. She was still relatively impoverished, but too proud to recognize her situation, renaming her lowly cottage 'Forresters Hall'.

It was not until 1984 that a turn of events would lead to a rekindling of the ambition to realize the capital tied up in Heath House.

* * *

Simon Dale's body arrived at Hereford mortuary at half-past midnight and the lengthy process of a murder autopsy began. The video crew, who had carefully recorded the scene at Heath House, set up their equipment to film the proceedings and Peter Acland stood aside as Norman Weston carefully noted external details. Having removed clothing from the body they set about obtaining samples for future comparison: adhesive tape applied to every inch of skin, to identify foreign fibres, hairs, or debris which may have been left by the killer; hair samples taken from the head, eyebrows and pubic area; and scrapings gleaned from beneath the fingernails which might reveal fragments of blood or skin if he had fought with his assailant. Glass phials containing samples were soon spread over an adjacent table, where an exhibits officer worked into the night recording them.

When Weston finished it was the turn of Acland and Cole to examine the body. A pattern of injuries will often satisfy the investigator of a sequence of events, but the internal examination serves to establish which injuries caused damage to particular organs, and led to death.

On the balding head there were five deep wounds which were readily visible when the dried blood had been cleaned away. A slightly curved oblique wound ran 5 centimetres along the left forehead; a flap-like laceration, 1.5 centimetres long, stood high on the right forehead, almost on top of the head; on the back two long, straight wounds, each about 5 centimetres long, traversed the head obliquely from low left to high right; below the lower wound was a further flap measuring 1 centimetre long.

Apart from a small abrasion to the left index finger there were no injuries to the hands. In particular there were no defence wounds. At a later examination further minor bruising was apparent over the left elbow, left upper arm and right outer thigh.

The head wounds were deep – they had cut through the scalp – but the skull was undamaged. The blows had been hard, but not devastating – probably enough to stun and subdue, but not necessarily to knock out cold. Dale's brain was uninjured, and it could be safely concluded that he had not died from the blows to his head.

The airways and lungs were clogged with aspirated blood

and exploration of deep bruising in tissues round the neck revealed the shattered remnants of the larynx, or voice box.

'Well, this is it: he's had a localized bash across the larynx and choked on his own blood.'

'A karate chop?'

'Possibly, but I'm more in favour of something narrower, longer, harder...'

Another voice in the background: 'Like a poker?'

'Yes, something like that, something rod-like...'

Norman Weston had also reached a conclusion. 'That arc of blood spattering on the table, that must have been after he was hit across the neck. The spattering would fit very nicely with someone coughing and spluttering with a throat full of blood.'

When the task was complete it was almost four in the morning; it had not been pleasant. Such occasions never are, but the heavy, pungent smell of putrefaction made this one even worse. Cole guessed he was asking the impossible:

'Any more on time of death, Peter?'

His colleague gave a wry smile: 'You've been in that kitchen and experienced the heat. It would have been warmer still before the doors were opened. It's impossible to say except that he would certainly have been lying there longer than twelve hours. You're the detective – you'll have to rely on your powers of deduction.'

Cole's retort is unprintable, but Acland's ironic reply was well aimed at the detective's retreating back as he headed for the door. 'One thing's for sure though – we're dealing with a murder.'

By the time Cole received a report from Matthews about his visit to the baroness and made arrangements for the following day it was hardly worth the journey home. During a couple of hours' fitful sleep a thousand and one things raced through his mind before he returned to Heath House shortly before ten o'clock. There was a bustle of activity around the place. Newspaper and television people were arriving in force and much of his morning was taken up with meeting their insatiable demands. Already they were murmuring about a possible connection with the killing of Hilda Murrell three and a half years before. Cole groaned at the very thought. He could never reconcile himself to the expectations of reporters who wanted a complete analysis and instant solution to a situation within hours of its occurrence. They never seemed to acknowledge the need for painstaking accuracy, and he already anticipated that if the answer to this one was not immediately forthcoming he was in for a difficult time. The remoteness of the area would be unlikely to produce many eye-witnesses.

Detective Superintendent Ian Bullock had been summoned to run the routine aspects of the inquiry. He sat in splendid isolation in a mobile office at the side of the driveway. Not the most patient individual, the fiery redhead was fuming at his inability to get things moving. As yet he had no telephone, and wireless communication was affected by what is euphemistically known as a 'black spot'. In other words, it did not exist. The handful of detectives awaiting his arrival had been sent 'door knocking' – house-by-house enquiries in the surrounding area to glean information about the deceased, his movements and habits. Bullock knew that he needed many more men and there was an urgent need to find somewhere to base a computer and the staff to service it. He was also restricted by lack of information: his briefing in the early hours had been little more than to attend a murder scene where an elderly man had been battered about the head. It had been a shock when he turned into the driveway and saw the apparent splendour of Heath House.

When Matthews arrived he sat with Cole and Bullock in the cramped caravan, going over the events of the previous eighteen hours and planning the strategy of the inquiry. As they did so people began to arrive and it soon became clear that Simon Dale had not led such an isolated existence. There were many friends who, on hearing news of his death, offered assistance, bringing stories of the peculiar life he had endured.

One of the first to make contact was Jo Corfield, the most recent reader provided by the Royal National Institute for the Blind, who lived in the nearby village of Leintwardine. Although often mesmerized by Dale's verbose theorizing she admired his strength of character and independent spirit, and was also taken by his old-world charm. Jo had worked with him throughout the previous Friday afternoon and knew that he was expecting visitors during the evening. Dale had been trying to get people interested in developing Heath House as a cultural centre, but she did not know if the guests were connected with the idea; he was, however, unusually excited at the prospect of company.

Cole had heard enough of Dale's eccentric behaviour to whet his appetite for more. Leaving Matthews with a list of jobs, he and Bullock set out for Jo Corfield's house. She proved a mine of information – not only about the man's character and his relationships, but intimate details of his daily routine that would help establish the time he met his death.

Dale had been taken by a friend to visit his osteopath on Friday morning and on the return journey the car broke down in the village of Leintwardine. He telephoned Jo and she gave him a lift home. As usual they worked in the kitchen, aware from time to time of the presence of Susan and two of her children, Marcus and Sophia, about the grounds. Over the months she had become accustomed to them painting, or gardening, as she listened to Simon's tribulations and typed numerous letters to lawyers about his disputed occupation of the house.

She often did Dale's shopping and thus became aware of his precise routine. A comparison between the amount of food remaining in the house with what she had bought, together with the evidence that he was preparing his evening meal when he died, indicated that he almost certainly met his death late on the Friday evening.

When Jo Corfield left the house at about 5 p.m. Dale prepared to walk into the village to buy fresh vegetables from a cottager. She had no fears for his safety, for everyone in the locality was used to the tall blind man striding along the lanes, often in the middle of the road, with white hair flowing in the breeze and head held high.

Tracing the visitors was an easy matter as Susan de Stempel had taken the number of their vehicle. It was nevertheless a considerable shock to its elderly owner when he found police officers on his doorstep wanting to question him about his movements. In his early seventies, Ben Scott is slim, fit, articulate and interesting; he oozes urbanity and refinement. Shrewsbury was only a temporary home while he helped to establish a new venture in alternative medicine. There he met Susan Evans, a divorcee with two small children, who had previously been engaged as a reader by Simon Dale.

Recovering from the fright that he might be regarded as a murder suspect, he explained that he had never met Dale before the Friday evening. Their common interest in both architecture and Camelot had caused Susan Evans to suggest they made contact. The couple, along with Susan's children, arrived at Heath House shortly before six and as they drew up at the rear of the house a woman appeared at the window of Ben's caravanette. Her eyes blazed and she exuded hostility.

'What are you doing here?'

Susan Evans's reply probably aggravated the situation by its lack of deference.

'Are you Susan?'

A tirade followed.

'You must be the famous visitors. I'm the mad wife – or so he thinks. He's mad too. The house is filthy and swarming with fleas. Anyway, he'll be out in a month.'

The angry baroness strode away, but the incident so unnerved the couple that Ben took the precaution of setting the burglar alarm on his vehicle.

Ben Scott found Dale a 'thoroughly civilized and engaging conversationalist' and they chatted happily over a glass of sherry, while Susan entertained the children. She saw the baroness and two younger people in a huddle on the front lawn, and later saw one of these – a young woman – hauling a pot of paint on a long rope to the top of a large scaffold tower at the back of the house.

As dusk fell, the two men visited the cellars to view the 'evidence' of the remains of an ancient settlement. Passing in front of a ground-level passage window Ben was startled by another intervention from the baroness, who had obviously stalked them around the house. Dale stopped to close the window, but it was immediately pushed open again and the baroness barked: 'Do not close the window – I've opened it to let in fresh air. It's horribly musty in there.'

There was an embarrassed silence before Simon told his guest to ignore the intervention; his ex-wife always objected to his visitors.

Dale's disappointment was obvious when shortly afterwards Ben and his friend took their leave. The onset of darkness and the children's bedtime were the reasons given, but they were unsettled by the hostile atmosphere. As they said their farewells at a rear door the baroness and Marcus were hiding behind a stone buttress listening to every word. Their previous practice of sneaking into the house to eavesdrop on Simon Dale's conversations had perhaps been frustrated by Susan Evans and her children wandering around the house all evening. They usually knew what visitors to the house were about; this time they had no idea.

The pair emerged from their hiding place and, they told detectives, drove home as Simon Dale made his way through the rear rooms of the house towards the kitchen. On the way he removed the sherry glasses from the lounge, then set about preparing his evening meal. He made toad in the hole and went on to prepare potatoes and green beans. He poured himself a sherry in a fresh glass as he worked. With the main dish safely in the oven he was about to slice the beans when he heard a knock on the outside door. He was security-conscious so would no doubt have enquired about the caller's identity. Unlocking the door, he was within seconds of oblivion.

By Monday evening the murder inquiry was well under way, as evidenced by road blocks outside Heath House and officers checking all passing vehicles for information; others were calling at every house in the vicinity. Less obvious were the visits to Dale's friends and aquaintances. The debriefing of the baroness and her children had started; they were the most regular visitors to the house in recent months and were the most likely source of information about visitors and events. Cole wanted more information about family relationships and the dispute over the house.

Bullock was relatively fresh and worked into the night. Cole was tired but had one job to finalize before he could sleep. He had to ensure attention to detail in the scientific examination of the huge house. One ground-floor room, which was cluttered and strewn with masses of books, magazines and correspond-ence interested him in particular. Keeping carefully to roped-off walkways, he set the task. Jo Corfield had told him about the acrimonious correspondence Simon enjoyed with a variety of people and examination of it might establish a motive.

'Get a team to go through this lot. Start from the most recent and work back. I want to know if he had any enemies.'

Fourteen scientific officers would spend six weeks complet-ing the task Cole gave them that first night. When they had finished Dr Norman Weston would be able to plot the sequence of the attack; others' efforts would establish the time Dale died. No provable scientific evidence was ever discovered to assist in the identification of the assailant.

Cole's insistence upon an immediate examination of the contents of Dale's library produced results. Within days it opened up the inquiry in many different directions and eventually led to the discovery of a completely separate web of dishonesty. In the future, Cole would face the accusation that he had suffered from tunnel vision and settled upon the first suspects to come within his sights. The criticism took no account of the 1,700 lines of inquiry he pursued and the 3,200 people interviewed in the course of eliminating suspects.

Cole returned the following morning and drove past Heath House to Bedstone village hall where the inquiry teams and incident room staff were now based. Walking into the corrugated iron building, he was astonished by the hopeless conditions: a dozen women sat in front of computer screens trying to concentrate; others were answering a bank of telephones at the far end of the room; senior detectives briefed junior officers in another corner. Every movement was amplified by the sprung wooden flooring. It was bedlam.

The only place he could get some peace was the mobile canteen, parked in an adjacent farmyard. He sent the cook packing and settled down with his senior colleagues to assess developments. The conversation lasted well into the evening. The interviews with Susan de Stempel and three of her children took up much of the time, for their personal histories and accounts of the previous weekend were revealing. Simon, who openly disliked his father, was the only one who avoided the family troubles as he made his way in the wider world. The older brothers Alexander and Sebastian, based in Tokyo and London respectively, had distanced themselves from the dispute while maintaining contact with their father.

It had been left to Marcus and Sophia to assist their mother when she decided to spruce up Heath House with renewed enthusiasm to evict her ex-husband. Dale had been as obstructive towards their efforts as he had been to prospective purchasers. He refused to allow access to repair or decorate the interior and they had to content themselves with improving the garden and painting the outside. They worked conscientiously, often seven days a week.

Susan's confrontational nature and Dale's bloody-minded obstinacy inevitably led to disputes. The pair were prone to resort to the law and solicitors' letters flew between them. On odd occasions, the confrontations were violent; Susan assaulted him on two occasions in defence of 25-year-old Marcus!

She became aware of Dale's efforts to frustrate her when he began to solicit interest in the development of the site, and she made it her business to find out as much as possible about his affairs. She had two willing lieutenants in Marcus and Sophia. Despite locked windows and doors they found a way into the house through a passageway window. For months they rifled his mail and eavesdropped on their father; Sophia became particularly adept at creeping about in stockinged feet, hiding in a nook on the staircase to listen to conversations. It was no wonder Susan was able to lie in wait for visitors; she always had prior knowledge of his arrangements.

While the historical backcloth of the dispute was important, the family's inquisitors were more interested in the events of the fateful weekend. The three worked at Heath House throughout Friday – Sophia painting, Susan and Marcus gardening. Jo Corfield arrived at lunchtime and they saw her leave at about five o'clock. Dale left shortly afterwards – no one spoke to him – and returned with something in a carrier bag. Then a caravanette arrived with a couple and young children. Susan was annoyed by yet more visitors, but her account of the confrontation differed substantially from the one given by Ben Scott.

None of the family gave any explanation for being at Heath House during the evening when it was normal for them to leave at teatime. Sophia did not stay as long as her mother and brother; in the drizzle and deepening gloom she got fed up and went home to cook supper. Marcus said he stayed because his mother would never be alone at Heath House for fear of violence from Dale.

Having seen Ben Scott off the premises the pair left, Marcus assisting Susan to reverse her car out of the garage in the courtyard. She always parked in the garage as she didn't want Dale to know she had a new car – purchased, Marcus said, from a windfall on the Premium Bonds.

At five o'clock the next morning Marcus and Sophia left Forresters Hall to attend a wedding in Kent. Later Susan de Stempel persuaded her youngest son Simon to accompany her to Heath House with some building equipment. Simon, who had more important things to do, drove their large van and Susan travelled separately in her estate car. The delivery completed, Simon drove off, leaving his mother alone. She parked her car in the courtyard and decided to complete one or two chores. She visited the beehives in the walled garden at the far end of the house and said at first, that she had walked past the rear lobby and returned the same way. She did not notice the closed shutters in the kitchen or the electric light shining through the lobby window. Later she changed her mind and said that she walked around the front of the house, so would not have had the opportunity to see either.

A passing motorist later told Cole that a large estate car was parked at the front of the house at this time.

In the afternoon she made another visit, this time to take around some ladders. She went to the beehives again; it was a windy day and having put a brick on top of one hive in the morning it was necessary to repeat the procedure on another in the afternoon. Again she was at Heath House alone.

Meanwhile Marcus and Sophia were many miles away in Kent. They were late for the wedding, having made a detour to the village of Wateringbury to view the home of a female friend of their mother's former second husband, the Baron de Stempel. They travelled twenty miles out of their way to do so. They were also late arriving for the reception, without offering an explanation. It was late evening when they returned home.

On Sunday the family decided, unusually, not to work at Heath House even though it was a fine day. They spent the morning on domestic chores, burning rubbish on a bonfire and, for the first time in ten years, sweeping the chimney. Susan busied herself with a large wash and burnished a companion set. The poker was the one Matthews found in her car; she said it had been taken from Heath House months before and matched a set of tongs still in the hearth of the morning room. Simon Dale's home help said she was certain she had seen the poker there a couple of weeks before his death.

A visit to Worcester during the afternoon rounded off a family Sunday until Matthews and Clark arrived in the early hours.

Cole listened intently to the various officers who had interviewed the family. Suddenly Derek Matthews interrupted: 'There's something that doesn't gel here, Gaffer. This baroness and her kids go on about how poor they've been for years, yet they've all got newish vehicles and the cottage is stuffed with antiques – real good stuff. I've also had a look around the cottage next to the mansion, which they used as a work base. It's all been redecorated. There's a stack of good-quality antiques in there.'

One of the interrogators intervened: 'She's supposed to have won the Premium Bonds.'

Matthews was not convinced. 'Well she must have hit the bloody jackpot. She's spent a small fortune on the work she's done at Heath House. All the garden machinery is new and that huge scaffold tower wouldn't come cheap.'

But his concern centred not only on the unexplained possessions; he had been doing some ferreting around. 'I've had a chat around the nick and Susan de Stempel is not exactly unknown to us. In 1979 when she was called Susan Wilberforce she gave evidence at a coroner's inquest into the death of a male friend. Then a couple of years ago the uniform boys were called to a "domestic" at her cottage. She and her second husband – the Baron – had fallen out. It ended up with him being arrested, but nothing came of it – he was just put on the train back to London.'

Another interruption: 'Perhaps he's loaded and she gets her money from him.'

Susan Wilberforce had been innocently caught up in the tragic death of her friend, Louis 'Woody' Wood. In the mid-seventies she had become interested in flying and he was the chief instructor at the local club. Everyone in the district knew Woody. In his late sixties, twenty years Susan's senior, he had led the 'Biggles' life – twenty thousand flying hours under his belt and a personality to match. The hard-drinking old charmer formed an immediate friendship with his new pupil. Shortly after Christmas in 1979 his car stalled when crossing a ford in spate, and he died from exposure while trying to reach his caravan on the nearby airfield. The car belonged to Susan Wilberforce, and she gave evidence of ownership at the inquest.

The second incident Matthews mentioned was more bizarre. Some months after filing a divorce petition Baron de Stempel visited Docklow to recover some property. It was an acrimonious weekend and eventually all his clothes finished up on the lawn; in return he smashed a few plates. Susan locked him in the house and he escaped through a side window into the arms of police officers summoned by Susan. Her allegations about his sanity did not hold up when he was examined by the police surgeon and, after cooling his heels in the police station, he made his way back to London.

After so many years Cole thought he knew all about human foibles and devious behaviour, but he listened to the stories about this lot with increasing incredulity.

The conference was then briefed on the preliminary

examination of documents in Dale's library. Simon Dale sincerely held to his obtuse theories, but his inability to convince others increasingly frustrated and annoyed him. This led to acrimonious correspondence with numerous medical and archaeological authorities. Cole had asked his assistant to search for potential enemies and the officer summed it up in a few words:

'He seems to have insulted some of the best possible people.'

But he had discovered a far more important document than any number of hostile letters: a copy of an affidavit of means sworn by Susan de Stempel the previous year. Sworn on oath, it served to prove that her total wealth amounted to £800 in cash, plus Premium Bonds valued at £10. The document had been sent to Dale during renewed attempts to reach a settlement over Heath House and the question of his eviction.

Derek Matthews listened intently; his mind went back again to his midnight visit to Forresters Hall Cottages. The baroness told him she had largely relied upon the generosity of relatives to keep herself and the children going through many difficult years; but the house was stuffed with antiques and the driveway littered with newish vehicles. It didn't tally with the hard-luck story and this new piece of paper indicating penury. She seemed to have come into some money pretty quickly. Then he remembered correspondence lying around the cottage addressed to a Lady Illingworth. Who was she? Could she be a benefactor? Matthews raised this with the team.

His intervention completed the debriefing, and directions were now required. Cole was explicit: 'Carry on with the door knocking and roadblocks. Someone will know something and we've got to find them. Ask the baroness and her kids to come back in and explain some of the queries we've raised. We can also start talking to the people identified in all the correspondence, but I'm particularly interested in this Baron and Lady Illingworth. Get both of them seen straight away.'

Cole's last job for the day was to examine a collection of implements. He selected a metal bar, shaped like a chisel at one end and hooked at the other. Herbie had been specifically asked to look for anything which could have been used as the weapon described in general terms by Peter Acland.

'Where did you find this case opener, Herb?'

'On a hook behind a door in the cottage at Heath House where they kept their tools. It looks almost new.'

'Take all of them to the lab to be checked for blood. Then let

Peter Acland have a look, and see what he thinks of that one in particular.' It was just a hunch.

Two days later it started to rain and conditions at the village hall and caravan became deplorable. Cole held his daily conference in the entrance hall at nearby Bedstone School, where his staff could at least avoid the mud.

He asked for progress reports, and a young detective sergeant held the floor. 'Rob and I interviewed Baron de Stempel yesterday, Gaffer. He's something else. He gives you his life history and all his connections in five minutes flat. You can't stop him talking and he must hold the world record for name dropping. He didn't have much to tell us that was any use really – just background – but you'll never guess what he insisted on putting at the end of his statement.' He turned to the sheet of paper in his hand: "I know nothing of the death of Simon Dale. As a gentleman, if I knew anything about his death that was connected with Mrs Wilberforce I would not inform the police." '

Cole rolled his eyes in exasperation.

Many epithets have been used to describe the Baron Michael Victor Jossif de Stempel. A High Court judge told him: 'Stripped of your airs and flowery language you are a con man.'

His barrister invited a jury not to consider him a dishonest man simply because they might think of him as a 'congenital liar ... a monumental snob ... [with] a reputation in shreds ... a hopeless and inadequate character ... a man without courage.' More down-to-earth observers describe him as the type who makes ordinary people dive for cover when they see him approach.

He is an insufferable bore, who has made snobbery an art form. The baron does not walk – he struts; his head lolls to one side in a quizzical posture. His affected voice, constant references to the position, qualifications or importance of everyone he mentions, makes him sound overly pompous. He was obsessed with rank and title from an early age. There are those who remember him only for his encyclopaedic knowledge of the *Almanac de Gotha* – Europe's equivalent of *Burke's Peerage*.

De Stempel is the son of a Russian emigré who allegedly

fought with the Tsar and fled to England in 1917. His parents divorced when he was very young and he stayed with his mother. After doing National Service he went up to Oxford for an undistinguished academic career. He only lasted a year, but it never deterred him from claiming he graduated from Christ Church with a degree in history.

During his brief spell at university he knew Susan Wilberforce's brother, although the latter has only a hazy recollection and dismisses the contact as an irrelevance. Through this tenuous connection he apparently met Susan. The meeting sparked off an infatuation which outlasted Michael's two marriages and Susan's commitment to Simon Dale before reaching fulfilment in wedlock some thirty years later.

De Stempel's adult life is somewhat obscure, particularly the aspect of his occupations. He may have been employed as a financial broker, adviser or consultant, but his own description of his monetary situation is far more revealing: 'All my life my expenditure has exceeded my income. I very often don't read bank statements – I tend to find them rather depressing.'

There is however no obscurity about his commitment to the finest forms of self-indulgence. He aspired to a position among the rich and grand – an aspiration which cost a great deal of money, and all he achieved was toleration rather than recognition. It was fortunate that he had an indulgent mother and monetary bequests from his father.

Michael de Stempel wished to marry Susan Wilberforce when they were in their early twenties. She found his cavalier exuberance good fun, but her breeding sounded a note of caution when it came to the full commitment of matrimony. However, charisma survived the years despite infrequent contact – and then, in the mid-seventies, they became emotionally dependent upon one another. Susan was in dire financial straits and Michael gave support despite the fact that he could ill afford it. With rekindled passion Susan Wilberforce set out her stall to marry him; but although grateful for her emotional support after two broken marriages Michael was a reluctant bridegroom. More matrimonial entanglement was the farthest thing from his mind.

The marriage was allegedly never consummated and Susan eventually learned he was pursuing a wealthy widow. As a result, she became all the more determined to haul de Stempel down the aisle.

He did not submit without a fight. Although agreeing to marry, he procrastinated when it came to taking the ultimate step. Susan arranged a romantic ceremony in Gibraltar, but he failed to turn up and she returned home alone. More entreaties led to a rearranged celebration in Jersey on 11 September 1984, when the knot was finally tied. Thereafter the reluctant bridegroom spent most of his brief union with Susan sleeping alone in a tent in the garden. It is a strange coincidence that Simon Dale met his death on the third anniversary of the wedding.

There can only be educated speculation as to the true reasons why Susan pursued an unsatisfactory relationship to the point of matrimony. A fallacious theory suggests she married the Baron for the title she always coveted. Without doubt, she persists in using her noble prefix, but it is a foreign title with no official recognition in the United Kingdom. She would always have gained more credibility by the use of the maiden name to which she quickly reverted after her divorce from Dale. In the world of the British aristocracy, the name Wilberforce still counts for something.

The reason for binding Michael de Stempel as close as possible to her is probably more sinister than sentimental. She was spellbound by his charms in early years but had learned to live without them. Time, however, had done nothing to temper either her impetuosity or Michael's flair for imaginative conversation. His exaggerated rhetoric about high finance gained him an unwarranted reputation in certain circles as someone who knew what he was talking about; the better informed took little notice. Susan may have been one of those taken in by his impressive patter.

The elders of her family had cautioned against capitalizing on her father's estate, but the advice went unheeded and she lavished her money on the 'white elephant' of Heath House. Her brother reaped the benefit of his share and also inherited the majority of their mother's legacy. Susan had also confidently expected to be a substantial beneficiary but had been disappointed. She had to depend on smaller legacies and the generosity of others – living in impoverished circumstances when her ambitions were for a far grander existence.

Misfortune must have festered in her mind for several years and it affected many relationships with members of her family, who, if there had been no rift, might have offered even greater support. Eventually in 1983 she was presented with an opportunity to redress the balance and needed independent expert advice from someone with contacts in the world of law and finance. She turned to Michael.

A plan evolved, but as the time for action approached and the awful nature of its execution became apparent it was necessary to ensure absolute discretion. Susan was well aware of Michael's verbosity and needed to tie him closer. In law a man and wife are treated as one and only in exceptional circumstances can be compelled to give evidence against each other. Was it extraordinary to suppose that she was pursuing marriage with Michael for that purpose alone? If so, it was part of the plan which went sadly awry as the reluctant bridegroom decamped within months of marriage.

The size of the investigation into Dale's murder outstripped the sparse facilities available at Bedstone village hall, and the nerve centre of the inquiry moved to Kidderminster, twenty-five miles away. There it would remain for many months as analysts sifted information in an attempt to piece together the jigsaw. Cole and Bullock settled into the familiar routine of a protracted inquiry. Their practice was to keep in touch with the grass roots by debriefing the complete team at fortnightly intervals; more important were the twice-weekly meetings which they held with the half-dozen team leaders who controlled various aspects of the investigation.

Matthews was a key figure; the murder happened on his patch and he had a vested interest in success. Further interviews with the baroness and her children did not take matters much further. There were discrepancies in their stories, but these were not necessarily sinister. He was more intrigued by the aura of secrecy and isolation surrounding the family, and his brief was to explore their background. He started with immediate relatives and friends. While the officers deputed to work under his direction travelled far and wide, Matthews's attention was concentrated on the figure he had identified as a starting-point – Lady Illingworth.

He discovered that the Lady had died in November 1986 in a Herefordshire nursing home. The staff told him that she had existed on Social Security benefits, yet his officers were told by relatives that she was extremely wealthy. He was then told that a friend of Susan's had witnessed Lady Illingworth's will in 1984, but that the old lady had not been present at the time.

Matthews's detectives tracked down a massive movement of furniture and effects belonging to Lady Illingworth from a warehouse in London to a Herefordshire barn. Their discoveries started tongues wagging within the Wilberforce family and Matthews became increasingly suspicious.

It was a feeling shared by Cole at their next meeting. As if the complexities of the murder inquiry were not enough it now seemed that they had stumbled across what Matthews described as 'a bit of a fiddle'. He always had a tendency to understatement.

Lady Margaret Mary Clare Illingworth of Denton enjoyed, then finally endured, the extremes of human existence. Born into a privileged family she married a wealthy and indulgent husband. Widowed early in life, she became a gracious society hostess before ending her life, in the mists of senility, as a pauper with paper debts amounting to thousands of pounds.

It is impossible to find anyone who genuinely knew Lady Illingworth who will speak badly of her. Her position and riches made her neither patronizing nor aloof; she always retained a humility based upon strict Catholic upbringing and a spirit of generosity inherited from the moral influences of her forebears. The same plaudits will never be attributed to those responsible for her distressing final years, when she was in the greatest need of sympathy and understanding. It is an ironic twist that the chief architect of her fate was the person who received patronage, affection, support and companionship when she herself was lonely and in greatest need – Susan de Stempel, née Dale, née Wilberforce.

Lady Illingworth was the eldest of a family of three. Born Margaret Wilberforce at Markington Hall at the turn of the century, she maintained a life-long love affair with the place she looked upon as home. In her mid-twenties she fell in love with a man thirty-five years her senior, Lord Albert Illingworth. Unfortunately he had two distinct disadvantages as far as her family was concerned: he was divorced and an Anglican. These hindrances were, however, largely offset by his wealth. His title, awarded by a grateful government for services as a member of parliament and postmaster-general, further ameliorated any disappointment. His City directorships helped to distance him from his roots in the northern wool trade and placated those members of the Wilberforce clan who differentiated industrial from inherited wealth.

Margaret Wilberforce's strict Catholic upbringing did not permit her to marry until the first Lady Illingworth died and meant that she only enjoyed eleven years of Albert's companionship as a husband. The early years were spent at a newly acquired mansion at 44 Grosvenor Square in London. Albert lavished a great deal of money on its refurbishment and it became one of the most elegant centres of entertainment in the capital. The rich, the famous, the high and the mighty were received at a succession of dinners and receptions by the elderly lord and his vivacious younger wife. These were the golden years for a couple wealthy enough to ignore the depressed thirties, which foreshadowed the Second World War and unhappier times.

In the early years of the war 44 Grosvenor Square was vacated and the couple retired to Markington Hall where they contributed large sums of money to alteration and repair. During this time they saw more of John and Susan Wilberforce when they were home from boarding school, and after Lord Albert's death in 1942 the bond between Margaret and her niece became stronger. By that time the girl had lost her father and the pair found comfort in each other.

Margaret Illingworth continued to live at Markington for some years; she had a cottage on the estate which ensured her privacy. The widowed Mrs Wilberforce occupied the Hall and the two women always maintained a cool relationship. Cecilia Wilberforce was a gregarious, fun-loving aristocrat who was never at ease with some of the more stuffy and pious members of her late husband's family. She was also envious of her sister-in-law's spending power, although her breeding hardly allowed her to approve of the industrial source of the wealth.

A few years after the war Cecilia Wilberforce further distanced herself from the family by marrying a divorcee and thereafter leading the existence of a socialite. The marriage was significant for Susan in that she and her brother inherited the estate, and Susan, a sixteen-year-old adolescent, was drawn even closer to her aunt.

Margaret and her brother Robert never assumed legal responsibility for the children, but their emotional and financial support continued for many years. They often despaired as their headstrong niece bucked advice and went her own way. Eventually her attitude led to virtual estrangement.

The aunt was well able to provide support. She inherited Lord Albert's entire estate; the mansion in Grosvenor Square; the annual interest on a substantial trust fund; a couple of Rolls-Royce cars and all the family treasures. The ball she held on the occasion of her niece's 'coming out' in 1953 was the social event of the year. For several years 44 Grosvenor Square was again one of the finest establishments in London. If she had played her cards right Susan would have been able to live the life of a dilettante, but instead chose to forsake those advantages and married Simon Dale.

In 1967 the lease on 44 Grosvenor Square expired. By now it was the only privately occupied residence in the square and developers were queuing up to acquire it. Margaret Illingworth reached the heart-breaking decision to leave. All her furniture and treasures went into storage, while she moved in with her cousin Irene who lived in a spacious flat at York House, Kensington. Although she spoke continually about finding a place of her own, the flat became her permanent home. She never got round to buying another property, and there are many who believe that she really wanted an invitation to return to Markington.

For the next twenty years she was content to pay £400 a month to keep her possessions in store. It took four weeks for the removal men to empty 44 Grosvenor Square. Before they started a young estimator from a large removal and repository company, Giltspur Bullen, surveyed the task accompanied by her Ladyship. When they reached a basement strongroom Margaret Illingworth hesitated:

'I dread going in here. I haven't looked at our treasures since my husband died.'

That had been twenty-five years before.

A servant unlocked the door and the young man was immediately aware of the dank atmosphere. He tried the light switch but nothing happened. A member of staff brought a bulb and extension cable.

'I have never seen such a sight as I saw in that strongroom. All the shelves were packed with valuables and items were spilling onto the floor.'

He could not put a price on the contents but something attracted his eye which would put it into the realms of fantasy. In the middle of the floor lay a pyramid of twenty or so bricks, which he took to be gold bullion. Quickly making up his mind that it would be impossible for his firm to offer safe storage he

advised Lady Illingworth that she should seek the facilities of a
bank vault. He also expressed concern about the legality of
private possession of gold, but she seemed unconcerned and
said it had been a gift to her family for services rendered to the
country.

He was later told she made arrangements for the gold to be
taken to a bank. It had been wheeled through the streets of
London packed in boxes on a sack truck. The man who
allegedly transported the boxes to the bank is now dead and no
proof has been found of the gold's existence. The young
estimator is a sound, intelligent businessman, now managing
director of his company. Is it possible that the temporary
lighting may have played tricks on him as it reflected off the
treasures within the strongroom?

In her declining years, Lady Illingworth enjoyed an annual
income in excess of forty thousand pounds. She visited the
South of France several times each year and pursued her
life-long interest in the turf. She and Irene grew old together in
the large and increasingly gloomy flat, cared for by a faithful
old retainer, Kathy Whelan. John Wilberforce, now a
successful diplomat, visited them whenever he was in London
and they often received visits from other relatives. As she
became increasingly infirm Margaret's financial affairs were
handled by a secretary and legal advisers.

The pair were regarded with some affection as dotty old
ladies who squabbled among themselves but clearly enjoyed
each other's company. It was not until the early 1980s that
Margaret Illingworth began to display signs of advancing
dementia – and there were several who viewed them with
alarm, among them her driver for more than twenty years.
Albert Oslar had great respect for her Ladyship and in a
strange way, across the social divide, they became great
friends. After she had spent a spell in hospital, following a fall
in 1980, Oslar became increasingly aware of her frailty and
absent-mindedness. On one occasion when he drove her back
from Markington to London she asked him:

'Have you driven me before?'

He was certain that by 1983 the old lady was badly affected
by senility. There were others who were of the same opinion.

For thirty years Susan had had almost no contact with the
aunt who at one time was her closest confidante and

benefactor, but in 1983 she sought a favour. Her daughter Sophia, who was working in London, needed somewhere to live and it was arranged that she would stay with the two old ladies at York House. It was to be the beginning of the final chapter in Lady Illingworth's life.

In February 1984 Sophia took her to stay at Forresters Hall Cottages for what Kathy Whelan was told would be a fortnight's holiday. She did not return.

Another day, another briefing.

'We've got a bent will, Gaffer – but that's only the start. Lady Illingworth was a very rich old lady before she came to Herefordshire, but from all we've been told she was skint when she died. The bent will leaves everything to Susan de Stempel apart from one or two small bequests. The furniture stacked in that ramshackle old barn at Wickton is worth a fortune. We really should sort out who it belongs to. If it gets nicked and we haven't done anything about it there could be trouble.'

Matthews's concern was understandable, but Cole was becoming increasingly irritated that the Illingworth affair was detracting from the effort he could put into Dale's murder. He knew what he had to do.

Detective Inspector Mike Cowley headed the force's fraud squad. He had been selected for that position because of his accountancy background, but he was also a first-class detective, having cut his teeth for many years in the hard world of general crime. He also had the advantage of having worked closely with Cole on major matters in the past and the two men got on well together. He was the ideal person to investigate the Illingworth business. He was told to get on with it, keep Cole up to date with progress and seek advice when necessary.

With the two parts of the inquiry divided Cole could concentrate on his main task without becoming sidetracked by the evidence emerging about the 'bit of a fiddle'.

The drudgery of routine continued for several weeks, but patience and persistence were eventually rewarded. The full picture of the battle lines drawn between Dale and his ex-wife emerged during her attempts to refurbish Heath House and its grounds. The crossfire of lawyers' letters told a graphic and bitter story, but it was the accounts given by friends and casual visitors which stimulated most interest.

Dale's eccentricities had been discovered quite accidentally by a group of local gentry who felt some sympathy for his lonely, sightless plight. They enjoyed his extravagant personality and conversation. They knew about his embattled existence, and there were occasions when they themselves encountered the wrath of the baroness directly. There were often physical obstructions placed in their path – tree trunks and other objects laid across driveways and entrances. She invariably knew when they were due to arrive, no doubt as a result of eavesdropping.

To his small group of refined friends Dale was seen as a courageous 'uncommon type' – excessively pleasant and polite. To other, more casual, acquaintances he was a self-opinionated bore who could be irritating, arrogant, bitter and stubborn, particularly on the subject of his unsupported theories. He gave the impression of a typical eighteenth-century squire in his dealings with those he considered his social and intellectual inferiors.

Some of these casual acquaintances also had their brushes with his ex-wife. The husband of a prospective reader, hanging around the grounds while Dale interviewed his wife, was confronted by an angry baroness. Subjected to a character assassination of her ex-husband, he quickly formed the view that such an environment was no place for his loved one to work.

In August 1987 a businessman visited Dale with a view to participating in one of his schemes to open Heath House as a conference centre. It did not take him long to assess the project as completely worthless, but as he politely withdrew he saw his path had been obstructed by a wheelbarrow across the drive. As he went to move it Susan emerged from nearby bushes and he was given the same treatment. Any lingering thoughts he may have had about a business proposition were quickly dispelled as he beat a hasty retreat.

But it was the unfortunate Adrian Tindall, archaeological officer to Hereford and Worcester County Council, who had the most illuminating encounter. He visited the house in February 1987 after acrimonious correspondence with Dale about the value of the estate as an important historical site. The council's involvement had begun some time before, as a result of Dale's having lobbied local councillors and his member of parliament.

Letters failed to convince him of the lack of evidence to support his theories, so Tindall decided to meet him head on.

He had researched the correspondence between his department and Simon Dale and knew about the abortive test dig his predecessor had conducted several years before. The tone of Dale's letters did not fill him with confidence and, in the event, his intellectual honesty would not permit him to do other than confirm the opinions already reached. Leaving the house with a flea in his ear and threats of recrimination, he was ill-prepared for a further confrontation. Susan de Stempel was waiting for him.

She already knew the purpose of his visit. There was a veiled suggestion that her children had read the correspondence. She was anxious to know what he had discovered and, relieved by his honest opinion, treated him to a diatribe about the contested occupation of the house. She said Dale threatened to kill her and had dug her grave within the grounds. Tindall, probably influenced by his own recent encounter with the angry theorist, thought she was genuinely frightened. She pointed to an object she was carrying across her arm and told him that she always carried something to protect herself. He could not remember what the object was when asked by the police many months afterwards. Some time later he was shown a number of implements and identified the metal case-opener which investigators had found hanging behind the cottage door.

Acland received the range of implements recovered from the Heath. Knowing the importance of his task and the crucial nature of any opinion he might form, he pored over his notes and the photographic record of the dead man.

A long pair of tongs was quickly discounted. An ornate poker was a possibility ... it could have caused the neck injury, but he was not convinced that the sculptured handle would have left the flap-like wounds on the head without other features being imprinted. There were lumps of wood ... well, one might have left some wound or other but one piece would not be capable of inflicting the whole pattern. But there was also the metal case-opener, a short S-shaped implement, flattened at each end, one of which was notched, the other square. Acland rotated the bar and concluded that it matched very well. A couple of blows with this could have accounted for all the wounds to the head. He couldn't be absolutely certain, but it was a convincing comparison and the best possibility he had so far seen. It could also have caused the injury to the neck.

He arranged to have the bar photographed against the wounds on Dale's preserved scalp. The result was an almost compelling comparison.

The long-standing acrimony which existed between Dale and his ex-wife, exaggerated by circumstances in the months before his death, gave detectives a possible motive for murder. The belief that he had died on the Friday evening, when Susan and Marcus were the last people they had been able to find who had been at Heath House, presented them with the opportunity. Peter Acland's opinion about the case-opener meant that the means were also available. There was a long way to go, however, before conclusions could be drawn from the possibilities.

A fraud inquiry usually starts with one piece of paper. Fraud detectives follow what is colloquially called a 'paper chase', linking documents to evidence until the complete package of wrongdoing is presented to a court. It is a fascinating process for those with the necessary aptitude, but many detectives reject its intricacies in favour of the immediacy and excitement of general criminality. Lady Illingworth's story satisfied both descriptions, as a disgusting story of family treachery emerged.

The pieces of paper with which they started were two wills made by Margaret Illingworth. The first in 1975 was quite straightforward: her estate was to be divided between her nephew John Wilberforce and Lucy Kilfoil, an Illingworth relative living in South Africa. Ancillary bequests included a thousand pounds to Susan's eldest son, Alexander. No mention was made of Susan. The second will was made in 1984, when the old lady was staying with her niece; it left everything in trust to Susan and thereafter to the children. Again, smaller bequests were made to her nephew John Wilberforce as well as cousins Michael Wilberforce and the Right Honourable Richard Orme, Baron Wilberforce of Kingston upon Hull. The wording of the latter bequest was significant: '... in recognition of his having added lustre to the family name in this generation'. No one imagined Lady Illingworth using such flowery language.

The obvious upturn in the fortunes of Susan Wilberforce

dictated that the next step must be to test the validity of the second document. A will must always be signed by the maker in the presence of two witnesses.

Anne Devey-Smith met Lady Illingworth socially while she was staying at Docklow. She formed the view that the old lady was quite childlike, vague and confused. As an old friend of Susan's she readily agreed to perform the small favour of witnessing the will. The other signatory came from much farther afield. Father Joseph Dooley was an ageing priest who taught at Stoneyhurst College, a Catholic public school. A casual acquaintance of Michael de Stempel he was an innocent abroad when removed from a cloistered life and easy prey for the duplicitous baron. He was pleased to help and travelled from Lancashire to Docklow for the weekend.

Father Dooley arrived at Docklow on a Saturday evening. He did not meet Lady Illingworth and after a meal retired for the night. He was surprised by the smallness of the cottage, and indeed everything about the set-up seemed rather odd.

Before lunch on Sunday he was introduced to Lady Illingworth and they chatted for a few minutes. He found her very vague as she searched her memory for the names of Catholic priests she had known. Instilled good manners ensured that she found some matter of polite conversation to engage a stranger. After about ten minutes she was ushered from the room by Sophia Wilberforce, and Susan presented the priest with a document and asked him to sign at the bottom of its four pages. Lady Illingworth was nowhere to be seen and he did not remember her signature being on the document.

Immediately after lunch, with the unctuous thanks of Michael ringing in his ears, he made his way back home. He thought about the strange experience, but soon dismissed it from his mind. He was not a man of the world and had never been asked to witness a will before; all his close associates had taken the vow of poverty and had no need of such arrangements. Christian teaching combined with a cloistered existence do not stimulate suspicion. For this reason it was a stroke of genius to involve him as an innocent accomplice to the plot; a man of the cloth would surely withstand any scrutiny.

The recruitment of Anne Devey-Smith traded on years of friendship with Susan in younger days. She arrived at Docklow on the same Sunday afternoon and was ushered into the small living-room where Lady Illingworth sat with Susan and Sophia. The baron paced the room. After a while Sophia tried to persuade her great-aunt to take a walk in the garden. After several rejections she changed tactic and successfully suggested a glass of sherry in the kitchen. Susan then produced the will and asked Devey-Smith to sign it.

In 1975 Lady Illingworth had relied upon solicitors who had served her husband's family for many years to draw up her will. The London firm of Theodore Goddard was long established and highly regarded. When she wished to change her beneficiaries it was strange that after many years of satisfactory service she should turn to the relatively unknown partnership of Mackenzie Patten and Co. of Twickenham.

Richard Sexton inherited Lady Illingworth's will from a partner who had been taken ill suddenly and found it necessary to recuperate in the United States. Michael de Stempel had made the initial approach, requesting that someone draw up a will for a dear friend, as he put it. Sexton took the matter over when the draft document was almost complete and within days received two typewritten letters. The signature on one purported to be that of Margaret Illingworth and bore the hallmark of age.

> ...please go ahead with the engrossment, just adding that in the event of my niece, Mrs Susan Wilberforce, predeceasing me I should like the residue of my estate to be shared equally between her five children ...

The second was from Susan Wilberforce:

> ...very grateful if you would be so kind as to go ahead with my aunt's Will as it is very much on her mind. It would be very helpful if you could do it on thin paper as opposed to anything thick. She has two phobias in life, one is the telephone, the other documents on thick paper. I do not know why this is, but she becomes very distressed when confronted by the latter...

Sexton did as he was asked. He never met his client and did not speak to her on the telephone. Although he wrote that it was unusual to draft wills on thin paper he none the less complied. The penny did not drop until years later. Lady Illingworth's signature was a forgery – which is facilitated by tracing from an original through thin paper. It is almost unbelievable that

Susan de Stempel managed to get away with such a blatant deception for so long.

While Cowley examined the secrets of the will his colleagues backtracked on Susan de Stempel's finances and others traced the recent history of Lady Illingworth's possessions.

Cole spent a lot of time thinking about the need for a bogus will if Lady Illingworth was penniless. As his detectives probed deeper it all became crystal clear. Document after document bearing the signature 'Margaret Illingworth' was returned from the West Midlands forensic science laboratory stamped 'FORGERY'.

When she left York House Lady Illingworth's affairs were in good order. For years she had maintained three bank accounts where she needed them: one near her London home: one at Ripon, close to Markington Hall; and one in Monte Carlo. In recent times she had infrequently needed the services of the Ripon branch, but within days of her arrival at Docklow she wrote to the manager asking for a cashpoint card to facilitate withdrawals while staying in Herefordshire. She had never required one before. In the following month £2,000 was withdrawn from the account through automatic cash dispensers.

Shortly after Margaret Illingworth arrived at Docklow Susan telephoned the housekeeper, Kathy Whelan. Michael de Stempel and Marcus would be calling the following Sunday to collect her aunt's clothing. The aged lady realized that the holiday was being extended and grew uneasy. She had not got on very well with Sophia during her stay and there had been one or two disquieting incidents. Lady Illingworth's handbag had once been mislaid and discovered under Sophia's bed. The secretary noticed that her Ladyship's personal files had been rifled; because of their confidential and intimate nature she informed the local police.

Kathy rightly smelled a rat and when the men arrived for the clothing she told them it was not ready. In keeping with his normal attitude when faced with obstruction by the 'lower orders', Michael de Stempel started to show off and threaten legal action. They returned two days later accompanied by a solicitor, who held two authorities' 'signed' by Lady Illingworth, empowering him to obtain all her property from York House and the National Westminster Bank in

Kensington. Kathy was bullied into releasing everything. The three men spent eight hours searching and clearing the flat; at one stage Michael de Stempel became so excitable that his companions locked him in the library. He was a confounded nuisance and impeded the search. They were obviously looking for something specific, in addition to the four boxes of neatly ordered personal documentation in the study. At last they found a box containing more papers and allowed Michael to examine the contents.

'This is what we are looking for!' he exclaimed.

They left with the van loaded and all traces of Margaret Illingworth's life at York House were effectively removed. The hijack was complete.

Now that they had details of all Lady Illingworth's affairs the embezzlement of her finances reached maniacal proportions. It was a well-planned operation. For the time being material possessions could wait; liquid assets were given immediate priority.

Michael de Stempel scurried around the 'old boy' network, trying to obtain the best possible advice for 'an elderly relative of a dear friend'. There were, he said, considerable assets she wished to invest, and was looking for the best possible tax advantages. He did not confine his efforts to the mainland; a letter he wrote to the manager of the Midland Bank Trust (Corporation) in Guernsey is an example of what they had in mind:

> ...if a joint account (in a very large sum of money) was opened by an eighty-four year old woman and her only niece with your branch, both resident ... in the United Kingdom, what ... would happen ... if the older woman dies – presumably the surviving account holder would continue ... and be entitled to continue ... to operate the account. My solicitor, Lord Coleraine, is extremely interested in your reply.

He could never resist an opportunity to drop a name. Lord Coleraine had acted for him in the past, but had not given de Stempel permission to use his name, nor had he made any helpful suggestions. On the contrary, he emphatically distanced himself from the baron's wild requests.

Enquiries were made about house purchase in the Channel Islands for tax advantages, but as Lady Illingworth showed signs of greater infirmity the plan was not pursued.

Susan Wilberforce made sure that funds were readily

accessible for any reinvestment. The documents from York House gave a complete picture of her aunt's finances. In double-quick time the 'forgery factory' produced a large number of letters and authorities. All Lady Illingworth's bank accounts were transferred to local branches in Hereford, then reopened in joint name with Susan. Another dispenser card was issued and £11,000 disappeared from the accounts through 'holes in the wall' in the space of a few months.

More joint accounts were opened in the Channel Islands and the Public Trustees were instructed to pay Lady Illingworth's annual income from the estate into them. In 1984 this amounted to £47,000.

Share Certificates, National Savings Certificates and Premium Bonds were encashed on forged authorities and a stockbroker quickly disposed of all her shares for £18,000. It was another easy matter to realize the £3,300 in National Savings Certificates and Premium Bonds. Great care was taken to satisfy the demands of the Inland Revenue: no potential pitfall which could lead to discovery was neglected.

The new will had been of paramount importance. When Lady Illingworth died it would be no good telling her relatives there was nothing left to inherit. They would want to know where it had all gone. Susan had to be able to prove the old lady's change of heart in order to legitimize her new wealth.

'FORGERY' was stamped on every authority detectives recovered. The case against Susan and Michael became formidable. But the police had only yet begun to scratch the surface.

When the assets were safely transferred to her control Susan had no further use for the incriminating records. A priceless historical record of the Illingworth family and fortune went up in smoke in the back garden of Forresters Hall Cottages.

The final duplicitous process could now start; the conversion of goods to liquidity. Susan's penchant for forgery was once again exercised to the full. On the basis of a sham authority Giltspur Bullen transferred all the stored goods in a massive operation costing £7,000. The bulk was transported to a rented barn at Wickton, while more select items were delivered to Forresters Hall Cottages. Lady Illingworth's gems were released by her personal jewellers on the production of a similar document.

Only at the National Westminster Bank did the conspirators

experience difficulty. On receipt of a forged request to release
the contents of the vault questions of liability and insurance
were raised. Sexton, the unfortunate solicitor, was instructed
to negotiate on the family's behalf. Susan told him that the
items were of little value compared to the effects that had
already been sold off to settle Lady Illingworth's gambling
debts!

Sexton accompanied Michael de Stempel to the bank, but
they were rebuffed by the management. The authority was
insufficient to empower them to release the goods. The alarmed
Sexton then witnessed Baron de Stempel at his best: 'He spoke
to the staff as I've never heard anyone speak to perfectly decent
people before or since.'

The neurotic Baron threatened them with the best of names
– Lord Wilberforce and the bank's chairman – but it was to no
avail. Within days more convincing authorities were produced
that finally satisfied officials, and Sexton witnessed the
handing-over of thirty-seven sealed boxes to Michael de
Stempel. He remembered some so heavy that they were as
much as two men could lift.

It was thereafter a clinical, swift operation. The best
sale-rooms in the country received the high-value furniture
and artefacts, and nothing was wasted. A portrait of Lady
Illingworth was torn from its frame because the surround was
more valuable than the picture itself. Susan and Michael made
several visits to the Channel Islands to dispose of the family
silver and jewellery at knock-down prices. Every vestige of
Lady Illingworth's wealth had to be disposed of so that the last
stage of the operation could begin.

The conspirators were well rewarded for their efforts.
Michael de Stempel was given £39,000; he would later say it
was the repayment of a debt. Sophia holidayed in Japan, and a
flat in Spain was purchased in her name. Susan, who admitted
to only two bank accounts when first questioned by detectives,
was found to have opened a total of forty-nine, in four
countries. Lady Illingworth's assets had realized almost half a
million pounds.

Susan's new financial status did not bring happiness,
however. The marriage to de Stempel was on the rocks almost
as soon as it began, and the promise of riches could not induce
him to stay. She also had the obstinacy of Simon Dale to
contend with and the increasing burden of a senile aunt. The
overcrowded cottage made life unbearable. Lady Illingworth

would have to go. Return to her relatives was out of the question, for she would be discovered to be a pauper.

Shortly before Christmas 1984 an ambulance crew was directed to Docklow. At the cottage they found a very confused old lady and two younger women anxious for her to be admitted to hospital. It was said that she had become aggressive and taken a hammer to the windows. There was no local doctor to ask so they took her to Hereford County Hospital. Since neither of the younger women volunteered to travel with the old lady, the ambulancemen assumed they would follow on behind. But Susan and Sophia had no such intention and did not visit for several days. Lady Illingworth could now be discarded.

The houseman who examined her diagnosed senile dementia. The once-proud lady did not know her age or where she was and she thought her husband would be working at the House of Lords. A psychiatrist said that her condition would have been noticeable for at least two years.

Lady Illingworth was in good physical condition, however, and the medical authorities tried to discharge her to the more familiar surroundings of Docklow to alleviate more mental turmoil. Susan would have none of it. The reasons she gave were many and varied: her aunt was an alcoholic; she was sex-mad; she had a penchant for hitch-hiking; they could not prevent her escaping; the house was overcrowded; and she had two children to look after (she failed to mention they were in their twenties). She wrote that the old lady was penniless and relied solely upon an old-age pension; it was about the only grain of truth.

> ...My aunt has had a very difficult time ... widow for over forty years.... She sold a very small house in 1946 ... all invested in Australian mines which went bust.... She lived with a series of friends until I heard about her plight.... She has no living relatives except me.... She has no bank or Post Office account or Premium Bonds....

Reluctantly the doctors made arrangements for her admission to Langford House, an old people's home maintained by the Local Authority, where she faded away for two years in abject mental confusion. Her stay was financed by supplementary benefit, courtesy of the Department of Social Security, and she

lived without any gifts, additional comforts or visitors; Susan
and Sophia went to see her only very occasionally.

Lady Illingworth was recognized as someone special by her
guardians; her natural dignity, bearing and manners set her
apart. Although becoming extremely fond of her, her carers
soon accepted that she was incapable of sensible communication and they never found out anything about her. On 9
November 1986 she died in her sleep. A basic cremation was
arranged, without flowers or memorial, and Susan, Marcus
and Sophia were the only mourners. For weeks the
crematorium superintendent unsuccessfully tried to obtain
instructions for the disposal of the ashes, and eventually took
it upon himself to scatter them within the grounds. The
unfortunate undertaker was never paid his account for £389.

During her aunt's stay in the nursing home Susan avoided
contact with other members of the family. Uncle Robert died
and she attended the funeral at Markington, but arrived in the
nick of time for the service and left immediately. She did not
risk the large family gathering at the Hall afterwards.

It was seven weeks after Lady Illingworth's death before
Susan contacted any member of the family. She said that she
had good reason not to do so, claiming that while going through
her aunt's papers she came across a tattered handwritten note.
Because of its condition she typed it out. The note, dated June
1982, detailed Lady Illingworth's wishes for her funeral:

> ...I no longer wish to be buried near my Husband ... facts have
> come to light that make this impossible for me ... now wish to be
> cremated privately wherever I die ... no announcement to be
> made in the press ... do not wish that any members of my family
> from Markington be present nor any members of my late
> husband's relations ... ashes to remain wherever I am cremated.'

Susan attached the note to the forged will when she sent it off
to the solicitor Sexton. He, like everyone connected with the
transfer and disposal of Lady Illingworth's assets, had never
been allowed access to her, either personally or by telephone.

The deception was complete. Lady Margaret Illingworth and
her enormous wealth had disappeared.

On 30 December Susan broke the silence. In a mendacious
letter to the senior member of the family, Lord Wilberforce, she
wrote:

...Aunt Puss died on 9th November. She went into a nursing home at the end of October ... very happy and beautifully looked after ... in a letter written in 1982 she decreed ... cremated where she died ... ashes remaining there ... no announcement ... no-one from Markington ... no Illingworths. In her Will she left ... and the rest to me. I do not think anyone will get any money because I do not think there was any ... Aunt Puss had terrible financial problems for years ... she came here with her affairs in a terrible tangle ... it was all finally sorted out and up to date.

The letter rambled on for page after page of platitude. Some members of the family were treated with flattery, while others were denigrated. There were some telling phrases.

the doctor ... could not believe Aunt Puss was 84, marvelling at her mental state and general condition. ... she regained her peace of mind ... to be able to retain one's dignity in old age is so important ... she kept every letter she ever had ... we had a bonfire going for about three and a half months ... she was determined to go through everything and get rid of it. Four crates consisted solely of sugar ... after 200 lbs I gave up counting ... three crates of scrubbing soap. Most of the things from Grosvenor Square had been disposed of at the time the house was vacated.

There was another letter in a similar vein to a distant cousin and close confidante of the aunt. The dishonest and cunning baroness was covering her tracks. In quiet moments Cole often ruminates about these letters. Why was it necessary to mention the boxes of sugar, soap and jam? Was it another decoy? He found it hard to believe that a rich, sophisticated lady of middle age had placed such items in expensive storage over twenty years ago. There was certainly something very heavy in some of the boxes from the bank vault and Sexton, the solicitor, was not the only person to notice the weight. The men who had lifted them made sure they were placed on the back of the lorry to cut down the distance they would have to be carried when they reached their destination.

After two and a half months' solid work it was time to put the evidence to the test. Susan de Stempel, Marcus, Sophia and Baron Michael de Stempel were arrested on 7 December 1987. For three days Cole and Bullock faced a bank of television screens as they watched recordings of the individuals, interviewed separately by detectives. They had no great anticipation that their stories would differ any more than those told previously about the murder of Simon Dale – and so it proved.

Susan was detached and disdainful, and tended to treat senior detectives like serfs. She answered a detective inspector's scepticism about one of her answers by:

'It was – it damn well was! – I assure you it was, and don't you say otherwise, my man – it was.'

She was unperturbed about the allegations of fraud. As far as she was concerned her aunt was not senile, but mentally alert. She had wanted Susan to have everything and didn't see why she should have to wait to die to realize the wish. Despite the fact that Mike Cowley produced over sixty documents and told her that each was a forgery, Susan repeatedly and imperiously informed him that she saw her aunt sign every one!

Marcus and Sophia maintained that they knew nothing of fraud, deception or forgery; anything they had done had been as innocent assistants. They were extremely fond of Aunt Puss and thought she was fit, bright and lively until the last days of her life. As far as the murder of their father was concerned they knew nothing.

Michael de Stempel was a different proposition. He had been arrested in London and his unfortunate escorts had to endure a continual harangue on the long journey to Hereford. They could not stop him talking. He regaled them with his life story and mentioned every influential person with whom he had ever brushed shoulders. If he was trying to intimidate them he was remarkably unsuccessful; they simply maintained an irritating silence. The poor man spent the time talking to himself – his bubble had finally been burst.

He proved hard work to interview. He tried to bluster his way through by evading questions, but as point after point was put it dawned on him that the detectives were not bluffing. He relied on the same defence as his former stepchildren. He had only done what he could to assist. The large sum of money he received had been a settlement of debt. He did have some difficulty in explaining the unseemly haste with which he had sought advice about the reinvestment of Lady Illingworth's funds and his involvement in the sale of her property.

Cole knew his strongest suit was fraud; indeed, it was almost provable without the interviews. He was however obliged to give them an opportunity to provide an explanation for their actions. It did not take him long to decide that they had not got a convincing one and to charge them all with conspiracy to defraud. He left a decision on what to do over the matter of Simon Dale until later.

He had just got home when Bullock telephoned with some news. The charge of conspiracy had come as a terrible shock to Michael de Stempel, and as he was being taken to a cell he asked to speak to a detective. Detective Inspector Eamon Croft was equally shocked when de Stempel told him that he had information to impart about Dale's murder. Croft was suspicious and careful. He told de Stempel he should not think it would get him off the hook.

Undeterred by the warning de Stempel told him that on Saturday, 12 September he had received a telephone call from Susan. She said that Dale had been killed. This was thirty-six hours before the discovery of the body. She pleaded with him to come to her aid at a time of such distress. He later received a call from Sophia making the same request. At the time of Susan's call he had been at the home of his first wife. Later in the day he went to his friend in Kent.

Sophia and Marcus had already told detectives that they visited the Kent village when they diverted from the wedding.

Bullock relayed the development to Cole and the senior detective advised caution. 'Be very careful, Ian – he's like a rat in a barrel. We must be sure he's telling the truth. If he sticks to this story be sure to get every tiny detail – corroboration will be essential.'

De Stempel stuck to his story, but after weeks of effort the murder team were unable to find a scrap of corroboration. Susan and her children denied having made the calls: Susan was most confident. 'You cannot prove I called him. I don't even know the number.'

An assessment of evidence available to substantiate charges of murder was undertaken. It was the responsibility of Crown Prosecution lawyers to make the final decision, and after many hours of analysing, heart searching, breast beating and no little vacillation it was decided to charge Susan de Stempel, Marcus and Sophia with Dale's murder. It was Michael de Stempel's crucial intervention which sealed the matter. Senior lawyers within the Crown Prosecution Service had a change of mind and withdrew the charge against Marcus and Sophia within two weeks of its preferment. Susan stood alone.

It was to be almost twelve months before Leominster magistrates were asked to decide if she had a case to answer. The best legal brains in the Midlands were engaged: two brilliant young barristers, both now appointed Queen's Counsel, prepared to engage in the preliminary battle. David Crigman presented the case for the Crown and Anthony Hughes represented Susan de Stempel.

Over 90 per cent of such cases are forwarded to the Crown Court on the production of statements and exhibits. In those few cases where there is a formal hearing it is only necessary to satisfy magistrates that there is a prima-facie case to answer, and Crigman set about his task with gusto. He relied substantially on evidence contained in statements, which he produced while outlining his case to the court. He and Hughes were, however, concerned about the testimony of the baron and the formal proceedings centred on that issue.

Michael de Stempel was called to the witness stand and swore to tell the truth. Crigman did what he could, but the baron was at his blustering best. Only one part of his evidence mattered: when did he receive the telephone call from Susan? If it was 12 September she must have known about Simon's death before she made the visits to Heath House. He was sure the call was made at 8 a.m., but because their voices were identical he could not now be certain whether it was Susan or Sophia; and he was unsure about the date. He could not say whether it was the 12th or the 19th. He definitely remembered his visit to his friend in Kent on the 12th – he had given the police the train ticket to prove it. All he could link Susan's call to was the purchase of a pheasant for dinner and that could well have been on the 19th. His value as a witness evaporated in a welter of infuriating vagueness.

The remaining evidence was, however, enough to convince the magistrates that Susan de Stempel had a case to answer and should stand trial for Dale's murder.

The trial before Mr Justice Owen at Worcester Crown Court excited the media, for it had all the ingredients they required: the rich and privileged in the spotlight; scandal, intrigue and violence. Only sex was missing. In truth it was no more exceptional than any trial for murder. In the course of eleven days witnesses gave their evidence while the mixed jury showed varying degrees of interest and concentration. Throughout, Michael de Stempel paced the foyer waiting to be called. He never was.

There were one or two remarkable moments. Susan de Stempel sat through the video recording of Dale's corpse lying in the kitchen without a flicker of emotion. She said that she had been taught to control her emotions. When being cross-examined, she said 'bollocks' to prosecuting Counsel, Mr Anthony Palmer QC. Her representative, Anthony Arlidge QC, almost had apoplexy, but fortunately Palmer missed the remark.

When Acland gave evidence he was led through the injuries and asked to consider what may have caused them. He acknowledged that he had been shown a variety of domestic implements including pokers, tongs, pieces of wood. By far the most likely implement compatible with the injuries found was the metal case-opener: the photographs showing the curved end of the lever next to the wounds were very persuasive, but Acland, with his usual caution, could not say that it definitely was the weapon.

He did express half an opinion that the blows to the head, if caused by such a weapon, were not done with a substantial amount of force, otherwise the head would have been shattered. Might that indicate a small woman was the assailant? He had to concede that that would be pure speculation.

Arlidge was no fool – far from it. He was one of the best lawyers in the country, and when the suave QC was making light-hearted comments about the pathologist's former boxing prowess, Acland was especially on his guard. Such a trick to divert the attention is a crafty trap for the expert witness. But one cannot say more, and one should not say more, than one is able. It was not possible to be certain about the weapon's identity – nor could one specify for sure the time of death. In themselves they might be regarded as small weaknesses in the case, but when added to numerous other missing pieces of the jigsaw it became more and more evident that the prosecution case was failing.

In his summing-up Judge Owen drew the jury's attention to the salient features of the case. He adopted the usual even-handed approach of a presiding judge. Could they without doubt be sure at what time Simon Dale was killed? If they could, it would be necessary for them to decide who was at Heath House when he was killed. Then they must consider how he met his death. Were they satisfied of a link between his wounds and Dr Acland's description of the tyre lever – and, furthermore, a relationship between the implement and the defendant's conversation with the archaeologist, Tindall? Was a loveless marriage followed by divorce, and further acrimony over the stubborness of Dale, sufficient motive for the alleged frustration and resulting explosion? They would also have to take into account the events of the Saturday, when Susan de Stempel twice visited the premises. Lastly he said that they would have to consider who would benefit from the killing in view of the evidence that a settlement concerning the house was reaching its final stages and that court orders would soon have been made about its disposal.

He reminded them that there was no scientific evidence to connect Susan de Stempel with the attack, nor had she made any admissions at any stage. There were also several red herrings about which only the jury could decide. A towel found some distance from the house, bearing stains of the same blood group as Dale, could not be connected with either Heath House or Forresters Hall Cottages. Vehicles and persons seen in the area at the time of Dale's death had not been totally eliminated from the inquiry by the police. Susan de Stempel had never been secretive about her movements on the Friday or Saturday; she freely volunteered all information relied upon by the prosecution to place her at Heath House at various times.

The jury was unconvinced by the prosecution's case and after lengthy deliberations acquitted the baroness. Waiting in the yard at the rear of the court to see her leave, they must have wondered why she was taken away in a van escorted by prison officers. Acquitted persons are supposed to walk dramatically from the dock to freedom! They knew nothing of the fruad charges, which had never been mentioned during the trial, and the police had been careful to ensure that the investigation had not been publicized. The Baroness Susan de Stempel was on her way back to prison to await a further trial.

The trial of Baron Michael de Stempel, Marcus and Sophia Wilberforce opened at Birmingham Crown Court in February 1989. Susan de Stempel did not appear as she had previously entered a plea of guilty to the charges against her. The judge explained her absence to the jury whose only task was to decide if the three persons in the dock in front of them were involved with her in the plot to defraud Lady Illingworth.

They faced an enormous task. The courtroom resembled a public archive; hundreds of files lined the walls. The history of each piece of paper collected during the investigation had to be proved beyond doubt, necessitating volumes of supporting documentation. It is always a long, laborious process and does nothing to temper public cynicism about delays in the legal process.

A stream of witnesses gave evidence about the methodical stripping of Lady Illingworth's assets and their conversionary benefit to the accused. Relatives, friends and medical experts testified about the deteriorating mental state of the victim. They had no doubt she had become a very senile, confused old lady before she moved to Docklow, totally incapable of managing her own affairs.

The three defended the charges on more or less the same basis. Sophia and Marcus had seen nothing unusual about their great-aunt's mental condition and believed she wanted their mother to have everything she owned. They knew nothing of forgeries or illegalities. Any reward they received was for work honestly done and they saw it as a duty to assist their mother.

Baron Michael de Stempel huffed and puffed his way through his evidence, testifying that he had been assisting Lady Illingworth, an old friend. He had tried to seek the best possible investment advice and to effect introductions for the most advantageous sale of valuables. Any money paid into his account at the time was reimbursement of previous debt, but he did not know its source.

The defendants' testimony was unconvincing and the jury found them all guilty. At last they were joined in the dock by the Baroness.

The Judge sentenced Marcus Wilberforce first; under the malign influence of his mother he had transgressed, though his role was comparatively minor – eighteen months. Sophia was more involved in the execution of the fraud and received considerable financial benefit – thirty months. Baron Michael de Stempel was a 'con man' who, though not clever enough to plan the fraud, had played a major part in its execution – four years. The actions of Baroness de Stempel were barbarous and wicked. As the architect of the fraud, she behaved with clinical coldness and greed – seven years.

Susan de Stempel showed no emotion as she strode from the dock, head held high. But inwardly she may have suffered a pang of conscience, for she was always intensely loyal to the illustrious name of Wilberforce and reverted to it after her divorce from Dale. When she became divorced from the baron she retained his title. Had she done so to avoid dragging her maiden name through the mud in the event that her misdeeds were discovered? If so, she had not anticipated that her two children would also be publicly blamed, and their decision to reject Dale's name in favour of Wilberforce finally rebounded.

6 Evil Abduction

The Stuart Gough Case

Richard Holden cycled home through the cold January evening little realizing that the events about to happen would, within thirty-six hours, leave him and another young boy emotionally scarred for life; another, little more than a child, would die. It was the weekend in 1988 when Stuart Gough disappeared without trace while delivering Sunday newspapers.

Richard put more effort into life than many of his contemporaries. He was a slaughterman who each morning had a long bicycle ride before starting work on the outskirts of Hereford at seven o'clock. In the evening he would return home late with little energy left for recreation. His shy, nervous disposition kept him mainly at home, a situation which did little to counteract his naivety. Richard was the youngest member of the family, and particularly close to his mother.

The eighteen-year-old got on well with workmates but his introspection and deliberate speech made him the butt of their jokes and he earned the nickname 'Zippy'. Outward appearances are, however, often deceptive and Richard proved himself long-headed, determined and independent.

On this particular Friday he left work as daylight was fading. He wore an inordinate amount of clothing against the cold: two pairs of trousers, two shirts, a tracksuit top, quilted jacket and anorak. Across his shoulders he carried a hold-all in the style of schoolchildren, with his arms through the carrying straps. His lumberjack's hat hid most of his features and, bent over the handlebars, he could have been mistaken for a much younger boy.

When he turned off the main Leominster road towards Wellington village it was already dark, and as he approached a

159

minor crossroads he saw the headlights of a car coming towards him. He took little notice as it drove slowly past but, a few minutes later, the same vehicle overtook him. Shortly afterwards it approached him for a third time and stopped. The driver, a vague outline in the darkness, asked directions to the nearby village of Canon Pyon. Richard recognized a strong Birmingham accent and later recalled that his polite directions had not been acknowledged.

Within a few hundred yards of home the boy was freewheeling down an incline when a figure charged from a lane on his left. Almost instantaneously the shape material-ized and a man, with unbelievable strength, grabbed his handlebars and stopped him in his tracks. He felt a sharpened metal blade at his throat as he was dragged towards a car. A cloth was placed across his face and he began to feel drowsy.

The next few minutes were blank before he woke up on the rear floor of a car being driven at speed. He couldn't move, but his head began to clear and he recognized landmarks near the centre of Hereford as he looked upwards through the side window. The driver never spoke and Richard couldn't move a muscle to offer resistance. Eventually he realized that the car was once more heading for open countryside.

For the rest of the journey he was in a haze. The car stopped and he heard a gate opening. He remembered nothing more until he found himself outside the car facing a powerfully built young man with dark features. He spoke for the first time.

'Where do you go to school?'

Still muzzy, he was unable to formulate a reply before drifting off again. Then he found himself being frogmarched across an orchard with a knife at his throat. He had been blindfolded and as his assailant gripped him tightly he was aware of a distinctive, disgusting body odour. He had no idea how much later it was when he came to again sitting with his back to a tree. He felt very cold and suddenly realized he was stripped to the waist. He felt a hand fiddling with his flies and the knife was still at his throat. Galvanized into action by a combination of fear and his captor's cold and perverted groping, Richard ripped the mask from his eyes, at the same time lashing out with his feet.

Luckily he found his target, surprising his captor, who still believed he was dealing with a schoolboy. Seizing the opportunity Richard took to his heels, crashing through a thorn hedge into a deep ditch of icy water. Convinced he was being followed he kept going across the adjacent field until reaching the road. He stopped briefly, heard no sound of a chase, so dived through another hedge into the opposite field, just in time to hear a car engine starting up. Crouching behind the hedge he watched as the car left the orchard and sped off along the lane.

Terrified and frozen the youth shook like a petrified rabbit beneath the hedge, summoning the will to move. Eventually he made his way back to the orchard and grabbed his shirt, before heading across more fields towards distant lights. He didn't stop long enough to replace his boots or outer garments.

It was just after eight o'clock when Richard approached a cluster of bungalows; he had no idea where he was as he pressed his face against a lighted window. The warden of the sheltered accommodation across whom he had stumbled got the shock of her life when she saw his dishevelled outline; fearing intruders, she locked her door and telephoned 999.

Constable Lewis found him wandering around the courtyard and listened to his garbled story. At Leominster police station he was reunited with his relieved parents who had been scouring the countryside, and for several hours was forced to relive his ordeal as detectives tried to obtain all information he could offer.

It took some time in the darkness to identify the orchard and it was not until the following day that the area could be searched for clues. Richard's outer clothing and boots were found, but there was no sign of his hold-all. An inquiry was launched, but the information Richard was able to give did little to assist in the identification of a suspect. He was unable to describe either the assailant or his vehicle in any great detail, and although he had been injured and traumatized, there were sceptics who cast doubt on the complete truthfulness of his story.

The following Sunday was intended as a day of relaxation for David Cole. For three months he had worked on an unresolved murder investigation and needed to recharge his batteries before giving evidence at an important trial the following week. He and his wife spent the day walking their dogs in the Cotswolds, returning at tea-time in anticipation of a quiet evening.

Shortly before six o'clock the telephone rang; it was Ian

Bullock, the 'on-call' detective superintendent. 'I've been trying to get you all afternoon. Have you heard the news?'

Cole pleaded ignorance; he had spent the day consciously avoiding current affairs! His subordinate quickly informed him of the disappearance of Stuart Gough from the village of Hagley earlier that morning. There was no reason for the lad to go missing and Bullock was obviously worried. He asked his boss to join him at the search centre in the local community hall.

Driving quickly towards Hagley Cole's thoughts raced backwards a few weeks, when he had presented the annual awards at Hagley's Haybridge High School and afterwards addressed the pupils. It was a splendid evening and he had enjoyed himself among the youngsters. He could not have foreseen, as he faced the sea of eager faces, that within a few weeks he would be responsible for investigating a tragedy involving one of their companions.

When he arrived he had difficulty finding a parking space. A large number of people were milling around among the usual trappings of a major police operation. He was immediately recognized by a number of press and television reporters who surged forward with their usual barrage of questions:

'Why are you here, Mr Cole?'

'Is it a murder inquiry?'

'Has there been a development?'

Stuart's disappearance was already a headline story.

Inside the hall groups of police and civilian helpers gathered around but his attention was particularly drawn towards a young boy talking to a policewoman. He looked drawn and under strain, and Cole took him to be a distressed friend of the missing boy. But Antony Dingley was recounting a story which would change the emphasis of the inquiry and eventually bring it to a conclusion.

The senior detectives were soon deep in conversation. In addition to the huge effort during the day to find Stuart there were two specific matters to report – first, the matter of Richard Holden. He was aged eighteen and he had been attacked forty miles away. His story was sketchy and there was no reason at that time to connect the two incidents.

More interestingly, information had come from the Cheshire police about a similar occurrence during the previous week. A young girl, delivering early-morning newspapers in a village near Chester, had been dragged into a car. Some hours later she was found many miles away in a forest ride in North Wales having been badly abused. Her assailant had not yet been found. Cole was soon on the telephone to his counterpart in Cheshire and arranged to send a team of detectives to liaise between the two inquiries. He then concentrated his attention on Stuart Gough.

Stuart was the much-loved and eldest son of Geoffrey and Jean Gough. A normal fun-loving boy, he was diligent in everything he undertook, and polite and easy-going in all his associations. In recent times he appeared to be growing out of childhood asthma although he had not yet gained enough confidence to leave home without an inhaler.

Like thousands of children he earned pocket money by delivering newspapers. His employer's shop was just yards from home and his round in the immediate locality. On weekdays he was away for about half an hour, but on Sundays the weight of papers necessitated two journeys and double the time.

Geoff and Jean had no undue cause to worry about his safety. Hagley, a smart, prosperous village on the fringes of Birmingham, is traditionally inhabited by the city's professional classes. In recent years it has expanded, but property prices are high and the quality of life remains unchanged. The close-knit community nestles beneath the picturesque Clent Hills, and the tranquillity is broken only by the incessant traffic along the main village road, which carries commuters from the western extremities of the Midlands towards Birmingham. Over the years, the only serious crimes have been committed by visiting burglars; other problems are a rarity.

On Saturday, 16 January Geoff Gough was working a night shift at a Kidderminster factory, about eight miles away. When he arrived home he went straight to bed and shortly afterwards heard Stuart going downstairs. He would normally have seen the child off on his round, but the family was expecting visitors and so he was anxious to get a few hours' sleep before they arrived. In the irrationality of later grief he was inconsolable at having missed the opportunity for a final glimpse of his son.

Stuart reached Malcolm and Gillian Higgins's shop at about twenty past seven. It took no more than ten minutes to check the first half of his round before leaving the premises. To reach his first delivery he walked past his home and turned into Newfield Road. He was never seen alive again.

The Higginses are conscientious employers, well aware of the responsibilities they owe their young charges. When Stuart had not returned for his second bag at twenty past eight Gillian telephoned Jean Gough to enquire whether he had been taken ill and returned home.

Malcolm visited all the houses on Stuart's route and confirmed that he had delivered every paper. None of the customers had seen the boy and there was no trace of him in the deserted roads around the estate. After frantic searches throughout the village Jean Gough contacted Kidderminster police.

Two local police officers directed to the house quickly appreciated the seriousness of the situation when they saw the distraught parents – this was no irresponsible youngster who had suddenly taken it into his head to skip off for the day.

As word got round, hundreds of villagers joined in the search. Immediate national news coverage brought many more to the area, which, in the process, created a logistical problem for the police commander. Without proper co-ordination there was a risk of the area being overrun by well-intentioned searchers who would not know precisely what they were looking for, and at the end of the day no one would know which places had been searched and which had not. Previous experience also dictated the need for proper control of the press, who arrived in large numbers. Matters eventually became better organized, but Stuart was still missing.

When the boy's disappearance was publicized the amount of information which reached the police was overwhelming. Although a percentage always comes from cranks, the majority is well intentioned but useless. The task is to sort the wheat from the chaff and prioritize that which may prove useful. Within hours normal facilities were deluged, and it became necessary to organize a fully computerized incident room in order to exercise some control.

While the future strategy of the search was being discussed on the Sunday evening Ian Bullock was called from the room and returned a few minutes later, his face flushed with excitement. Cole sensed there had been a development.

* * *

The anxious boy sitting in the corner of the hall when Cole first arrived was the cause of Bullock's optimism. Antony Dingley, a schoolfriend of Stuart, delivered papers for another newsagent in the village. His round took him by bicycle through lonely country lanes to the hamlet of Broome. On Saturday morning he had set off as usual just after seven o'clock along the Worcester road and turned into a country lane towards his first delivery. Emerging from a cottage path he saw a car coming slowly round a bend and stop alongside him.

'Can you tell me the way to Birmingham?' said the young round-faced black man. When told to turn right at the end of the lane he wound up his window and drove off without a word of thanks.

Half a mile further along the lane Antony saw the same car once more driving slowly towards him. The driver must have turned left instead of right, and for some reason the boy sensed danger and turned into the nearest driveway. He stood astride his bicycle as the car crept past the entrance the driver looked directly at him. The vehicle accelerated away and Antony pedalled furiously towards his next port of call.

Broome is a cluster of houses surrounding a triangle of roads. The through road traverses the base of the triangle, and there is no reason why the passing traveller should need to use the other two accesses. It is therefore not difficult to imagine Antony's alarm when he next saw the predatory vehicle passing through one of these minor roads as he was pushing a paper through a letter-box. It must have travelled in a circle yet again, and in the opposite direction to his instructions.

Although by now thoroughly apprehensive about the driver's motives his youthful reticence stopped him from raising the alarm. He thought how foolish he would be if there was some innocent explanation. However, apprehension turned to distinct fear when he saw the vehicle again – this time waiting at a crossroads for him to emerge from a farm driveway. Terror put wings on his heels as he cycled towards the sanctuary of a busy road, but before he could reach it he heard the pursuing car. Once again he dived into a driveway and this time hid behind a thick laurel hedge. The sound of the car receded into the distance, but he remained where he was.

With some alarm he heard a vehicle coming back towards him, but was relieved to see a postman drive past and pull up at a nearby house. With the protection of the post van he decided to go on and was just emerging from the driveway when his tormentor reappeared. This time he also obviously saw the post van and accelerated away. Antony rode to the safety of the main road and did not see the man again.

All this happened within a mile of Stuart Gough's paper round. It is understandable that in youthful innocence Antony told no one of his experiences; he did not wish to alarm his parents. He also wondered whether he was being unnecessarily sensitive. He knew he would be safe the following day because his mother always drove him around on Sundays. What his attitude might have been on the Monday morning, when he would have to retrace his route alone, is a matter of conjecture.

Antony's story was of great significance. A predator stalking a newsboy on Saturday, followed by the disappearance of another the next day, could not be coincidence within such a confined area. The priority had to be the identification of the man. The predominance of white people in Hagley ensured that a black man would be noticed at any time of day; hopefully by someone who would also be able to provide greater detail about his car. The urgent need was to get detectives on to the streets to find those potential witnesses.

Sunday evening became Monday morning and Cole knew he would have to snatch a few hours' sleep before his appointment in the Crown Court. He also knew that his commitment to that matter meant he would have to leave the Stuart Gough case to another senior detective for the next few days. Ray Steadman was the detective superintendent responsible for the Kidderminster area so he called and briefed him on his task. The two priorities were quite straightforward: find Stuart Gough and the car's black driver. Stuart's background and the grief of his parents made him keen to emphasize that the boy was not voluntarily absent. He was either held somewhere against his will or already dead. Cole left the hall at three in the morning with a heavy heart, almost convinced of the latter supposition. Nothing had been heard of the lad for twenty hours – he therefore had a shrewd idea of the poignant duty that would face him at some time in the future.

While driving home his mind raced over many issues, but he reached one conscious decision: he would stay away from the Gough family. Their consummate grief had been relayed to him, and experience told him that he must not get emotionally involved if he was to have any success in pursuing their son's killer. He had seen others make that mistake in the past.

Police officers had already been delegated to assist the family, and he would ensure they continued to do so for as long as necessary.

His decision was vindicated over ensuing days as Stuart's innocent face haunted every national paper and television news bulletin. Cole's youngest son was of Stuart's age and bore some resemblance. Perhaps, as a result, there would never be an event in his professional life which would affect him with the same emotional impact as the hunt for Stuart Gough.

Early on Monday morning hundreds of volunteers, marshalled by police officers, searched Hagley and its surrounds. More police officers visited every house and building within a five-mile area; mounted officers from the West Midlands police hunted the Clent Hills, while their colleagues in the underwater unit examined acres of standing water; helicopters flew over the area. The impact of intense activity changed village life and the community closed ranks around the Gough family. Worried parents accompanied their children everywhere.

The press corps invaded, interviewing and photographing anything that moved. The involvement of a newsboy concentrated their minds wonderfully and offers of rewards for information were soon forthcoming.

While the visible activity captured national attention a large team of detectives, including members of the Regional Crime Squad, had been assembled to chase any snippet of information which looked like giving a lead. The incident room collated thousands of telephone calls and prioritized them for further enquiry.

Two detectives had the urgent job of wringing every possible detail from Antony Dingley's story. He thought that the black man had been driving a Datsun car and identified a 'Sunny' marque at a local dealer's. He was sure it was a metallic silver colour. He was next taken to an artist, employed by the West Mercia police, who had the remarkable facility of being able to compile facial impressions from verbal descriptions. By Monday evening the sketch appeared on television news broadcasts and the following morning it was plastered over the front pages of the papers. This generated enormous public interest and several hundred people rang to say they had seen a black man driving a silver Datsun. The calls came from all over the country, jammed switchboards and completely clogged the computer system. The majority were useless, but none could be ignored until evaluated. The task of scrutineers was to find the one call which might hold the key to the inquiry.

More valuable intelligence was also being assessed. There are unfortunately a great many men who have paedophilic tendencies. The police know about those who have been convicted of such offences, but there are many more whose desires lie dormant until an emotional explosion causes them to fulfil their urges. It is the investigator's job to gather together all the intelligence about such people and identify his suspect. Again it is a process of identification and elimination within the parameters of available descriptions. Teams of detectives were allotted the task of evaluating information about hundreds of such individuals that reached the incident room.

The search for witnesses in Hagley bore fruit. Roadblocks gave police the opportunity to question passing motorists, while other officers waylaid pedestrians. At the end of the exercise there were three important witnesses. Between six and eight o'clock on Sunday morning they had seen a silver-coloured car prowling around Hagley: one said that the driver was black; another that he had dark tight curly hair. The vehicle was variously described as being white, silver, of foreign make and hatchback, as well as having a T in the registration mark and a loose exhaust. The similarities with Antony Dingley's recollection made the possibility of coincidence unlikely.

Late on the Tuesday evening Ray Steadman rang Cole with some potentially important information. Two calls had been received from reliable sources identifying a suspect. The first came from a detective constable in Wolverhampton who knew of a black man with a criminal record for attacks on young boys. Victor Glenford Miller was capable of the abduction. He lived with a white man, Trevor Norman Peacher, who had similar convictions. The other call was from a prison officer, who knew the same men from their time in prison and was aware that they had set up home together. Steadman intended to turn them over the following day.

He had one other piece of news to impart. Richard Holden's hold-all had been found in a field near Leominster. This prompted a flurry of questions but Steadman was as yet unable to provide answers. There was still nothing to connect the two incidents.

Cole tried to make his own enquiries but the detective

constable on duty at Leominster was not involved in the case. It was unreasonable to take the matter further at such a late hour, so he gave instructions for a comprehensive briefing at the Crown Court the next morning. He wanted to know every detail of the inquiry and, in particular, required an assessment of the authenticity of Richard Holden's story.

Detective Inspector Eamon Croft knew better than to approach Cole with half a story, particularly early in the day when his fuse was notoriously short. So he was well prepared when he reached the courtroom. Richard Holden's workmates had initially cast some doubt on the credibility of his story, describing him as a dreamer. Photographs of his minor injuries had been shown to Acland. They included various abrasions on the skin of the chest, some of which had been entirely consistent with the youth running or scrambling through a thicket without a shirt. A few areas showed more localized double parallel marks, especially an area on the left side of his back.

Acland had also been shown a broken piece of stick, one end of which had two protruberances which, when pushed against the skin, caused a double parallel line similar to those seen on Richard Holden. It seemed to suggest that some of the marks had been caused deliberately by an assailant, but Acland had not ruled out the possibility that they were self-inflicted. Was there anything else that could usefully be done to confirm the truth of the Holden story? It might have been possible to test his blood for traces of the solvent allegedly used to subdue the lad, but this would only have been useful within a few hours of the incident and they had long since missed that opportunity. In spite of the pathologist being unable to push the investigation much further, Croft was by now in no doubt that the youth had suffered a frightening attack, although he was still uncertain that he had been told the full story.

The most disturbing feature was Richard's insistence that he was, rendered insensible by inhaling an unknown substance. Deviants prepared to take such risks are rare and extremely dangerous. Croft was labouring under difficulties brought about by the insensibility, for the victim's recollections were dim and uncertain.

Progress depended upon close examination of clues found in the orchard, and there were several optimistic avenues. Training-shoe impressions may give a size and identify a manufacturer; tyre tracks can identify a make and measurements can be used to confirm a type or marque of vehicle. A minute flake of paint found on the gatepost might settle the car's colour.

Close to where Richard made his escape detectives found a new plastic dustbin liner, a whippy stick and several branches of gorse. At the time they could only guess that the purpose of such items was flagellation. The bin liner was examined for fingerprints; but a stick is a stick and gorse is gorse. There did not seem to be any mileage in further inspection of those items.

Richard's possessions were found several days after the attack in a field at the side of a country lane eleven miles from the orchard. His bag hung from a fence-post and his hat and gloves were neatly folded on the grass below.

Croft had found three people who saw a stranger in the area around Richard's home during the Friday. They noticed very little detail but spoke of a dark-skinned man with a round face who was wearing a woollen hat. They also remembered his dirty vehicle, which might have been a Japanese hatchback.

As the briefing progressed warning bells began to ring in Cole's head. Forty miles separated events and the topography was dissimilar; yet if one stretched imagination to the limit one could think in terms of the abandoned hold-all being on a direct route between the two abductions. He could not figure out the connection between the Welsh border country and the West Midlands conurbation; there were a thousand and one possibilities. He could only hope further effort would provide answers. When he left the court he tried to contact Steadman but he was out, 'turning over' the two suspects.

Late that night Cole's sleep was disturbed when Steadman rang in to report the events of the day. Miller and Peacher had been interviewed and alibied each other. They claimed to have worked together all week at Manders Paints in West Bromwich and spent the weekend in their flat. Enquiries with neighbours did not contradict the story; the men always kept themselves very much to themselves. They were confident and co-operative; the flat and vehicle was searched and both men were medically examined. Nothing of significance was found. Miller was half-caste and his car a silver coloured Colt Sapporo bearing the registration mark KNP 862 T.

Steadman expressed his satisfaction with the couple's story, but had not fully checked their alibi. By the time he got round to ringing Manders Paints events had overtaken him – if he had done so earlier, he would have discovered that the men

were not at work during the week preceding Stuart's disappearance.

On Thursday David Cole finished giving his evidence and
thereafter was committed to the Gough inquiry; he could now
devote his energies exclusively to resolving the issue. For the
remainder of that day and throughout the night he immersed
himself in the documentation of the investigation, reading piles
of statements, messages and policy documents. Little progress
had been made in the search for Stuart and some inspiration
was needed from the seasoned detective. He started to get a 'feel'
for two hypotheses – that the events of Hereford and Hagley
were connected and that Victor Glenford Miller warranted
further attention. In the early hours of Friday morning he
decided what he would do.

For some years he had been fortunate to work with his closest
friends and he now turned to one of them for assistance. Allen
Mayo, a natural detective with an analytical brain, never
missed a detail and was the ideal choice to assess the Hereford
inquiry. His evaluation during the ensuing weekend was crucial
in linking the sequence of events together.

Mayo focused his attention on the way Richard Holden was
stalked by the man in the car. A close examination of the routes
available to backtrack on the youth took the detective along
narrow lanes and farm tracks. His research pointed to the
conclusion that the abductor had spent considerable time
planning his attack, or already had an intimate knowledge of
the area.

Descriptions linked the assailant to the person seen hanging
about the district, but Mayo could not correlate the orchard with
the scene of the abduction or the route to the field where
Richard's clothing had been tidily abandoned. He began to
realize why Cole was getting edgy. He had intentionally been
told little about Antony Dingley's experience so that he could
keep an open mind. But he knew enough to see the similarities
and contacted his colleagues working at Hagley.

They knew about Holden and had satisfied themselves that
the issues were unconnected. Mayo was not so certain they were
right and continued his analysis. He knew nothing about Victor
Miller at that stage, but more particularly no one else yet knew
that Victor had been a residential pupil some years before at a
school in Bodenham, a village within a mile of the orchard.

Cole concentrated his attention on the two boys who had come face to face with the man he was beginning to suspect had killed Stuart Gough. For some years he had been interested in the power of hypnosis in stimulating memory and had used it selectively in serious cases. He made contact with Dr Una McGuire-Williams, who practised clinical hypnosis in her daily work. Her natural charm and confidence ensured maximum co-operation from her patients, and she was asked to see the two boys.

Cole's attention was then diverted to another development which rapidly assumed great importance.

Three years earlier a young boy delivering Sunday papers in the village of Pattingham on the outskirts of Wolverhampton had been abducted at knifepoint by a black man. Bundled into a large white van he was driven into open countryside and indecently assaulted. He secured his release by promising to tell no one about his ordeal, but eventually confided in his mother. She went along with his wishes not to involve the police but set about identifying the assailant herself.

The boy remembered a name painted on the vehicle and part of its registration mark. The mother traced the van to the Crypt Association, a community project based in Wolverhampton, and followed the black driver to his home. The next day she photographed him as he left for work. A contact at the Crypt told her his name was 'Vincent' Miller, but she still resolved not to tell the police.

Obviously, none of this was known to detectives trying to find Stuart Gough, but for some days they tried to identify an anonymous female who had telephoned Wolverhampton police earlier in the week. She was distressed by the similarity between the sketch of Antony Dingley's tormentor, published by the police, and the photograph she had taken of Victor Miller. They had made little progress until a man in whom she confided persuaded her to come forward. Cole quickly diverted teams of detectives to investigate the three-year-old crime.

On Saturday afternoon Cole and Mayo sat transfixed in front of a television screen: Richard Holden was under hypnosis. The effect was dramatic as he relived his ordeal and they were under no illusion about the authenticity of his story. He described his attacker and the vehicle in greater detail, but when he retold his escape through freezing ditches became distressed. In the centrally heated room the youth was shivering with cold, but the anxious moment soon passed as he was quickly roused from his trance. It was now clear why he had been unable to recall everything about his ordeal – his shocked mind refused to remember the reality of what had occurred. In medical terms he was suffering from hysterical amnesia or mental block, a symptom common in confusional states, which induces an impairment of memory for recent events. Richard had been confabulating or subconsciously inventing memories to fill the gaps. Under hypnosis such inhibitions were removed and the two detectives witnessed the full reality of terror that the boy had suffered.

From what Antony and Richard revealed under hypnosis there was now little doubt that they were talking about the same man. Stuart Gough had disappeared, so could tell them nothing, but the coincidences were too great. The black man must be the one who could tell them where the boy was.

Allen Mayo took Cole around all the locations involved in Richard's kidnap and they visited the field where his possessions were found. They then motored through Tenbury Wells and Kidderminster to Hagley. It was Cole's turn to explain the events surrounding the attempt to abduct Antony Dingley and show his colleague the route Stuart Gough took on the day he vanished. If they needed any confirmation the tour convinced them of the accuracy of their assessment. Within an hour of leaving Hagley Cole faced all the senior detectives involved in both inquiries in his office at the incident room.

He was infuriatingly dogmatic and assured: he would not listen to argument. 'Holden, Dingley and Gough are connected. Allen agrees with me, and we're going to sit here until we've ripped both these inquiries apart and found the link. Allen, you start and tell us everything we've got on the Holden story.'

It took well over an hour until he came to the scientific examination of the orchard. 'There may have been flagellation – a whippy stick and a piece of gorse bush were found near the spot where Richard escaped. There's no gorse growing in the area around the orchard so it must have been brought by the attacker.'

As he said this Cole noticed the expression on the face of a senior detective change from intense concentration to a dawn of realization.

'Bloody hell – there were some gorse needles in the boot of Victor Miller's car when we searched it the other night. They'll be in the bag with the other debris at the lab.'

Even if they had not yet succeeded in linking up the three inquiries they had just linked Holden to a suspect. Suddenly things began to happen and the pieces of the jigsaw started to fall into place.

Cole was warned by colleagues who had previously handled Miller that he was a difficult customer who would admit nothing. But the evidence was now building up against him. Miller and Peacher were proven liars – they had not been at work during the week prior to Stuart's disappearance. It is always a useful lever in an interview to be able to prove someone has lied while protesting their innocence.

Laboratory tests identified the tread pattern of a tyre mark in the orchard as belonging to an unusual Korean make. Miller's car had such a tyre fitted. Shoe impressions in the lane were made by Hi-Tec Strada training shoes, and similar impressions were found on the floor beneath Miller's desk at Manders Paints. Working closely to details given by Richard while under hypnosis detectives identified the car as a Colt Sapporo. Customized loudspeakers described by the youth were identical to those fitted inside Miller's vehicle.

The two suspects were quickly arrested, both of whom vehemently protested their innocence. For twenty-four hours Peacher continued to lie for his lover, while Miller maintained a stony silence. All the evidence was put to him in a series of lengthy interviews but he proved as obstinate as the predictions had forecast. The weight of evidence was formidable but he refused to budge. Victor Miller had good reason to keep quiet. If he was convicted of another homosexual attack on a youngster he faced many years in prison, and he was reluctant to sacrifice the only stable relationship he had ever known.

Miller's Jamaican father had been unable to cope with his two young sons when the lads' mother left home shortly after the death of another brother. The combined loss of a brother and mother affected young Victor's behaviour and the father's only antidote to his aggressive behaviour was physical punishment. That only made matters worse. Victor exhausted all efforts by the authorities to help him within the home environment and eventually was sent to a special school at Bodenham; he stayed for eight years.

Victor was an extremely disturbed child; his behaviour worsened and staff experienced difficulties in controlling his outlandish ways. His family hardly every bothered with him and he became increasingly introverted, spending hours cycling alone through the lonely country lanes. On occasions he would be missing for hours only to be discovered curled up in a foetal position in cupboards or under furniture – in a trance of his own peculiar thoughts. He was tormented by tidiness, spending hours folding and arranging his possessions. His territorial instincts were acute and he raged against anyone who invaded his personal space.

When he reached the age limit for the special establishment he returned to a state school but they were unable to cope with his conduct. In 1971 he suffered a complete breakdown and thereafter a pattern of sadistic behaviour began to manifest itself.

Bullying graduated to terrorizing, and Victor was soon before the courts. From minor offences of burglary and possessing weapons he quickly progressed to predatory behaviour. He was not caught every time, mainly because the majority of his victims were either too frightened or ashamed to report the attacks. When he was caught his ability to withdraw into the natural cunning of the psychopath made him a difficult opponent; he could comfortably lie or mutely resist questioning for hour after hour.

Probation officers and social workers could do nothing with him and he was sent to Borstal. In 1976, convicted of indecent assault for the first time, he was committed to prison for four years, a sentence whose length reflected the seriousness of his crime. He had terrorized his victim with a knife.

He therefore entered the university of crime in which thieves, robbers and perverts educate each other in their peculiar skills. He was segregated from ordinary criminals and spent his sentence with other deviants. He was well behaved, polite, clean and tidy – bonus points which earned him parole after two and a half years. He went to live in a gay community on the south coast, and within weeks the faith of those responsible for his early release was shattered. He attacked a sixteen-year-old youth at knifepoint and fled to Wolverhampton. But he was unable to restrain himself for long. He took on two young men with his knife, sadistically stabbing one of them in the chest, and was soon back in prison on a seven-year sentence.

A fellow prisoner seduced young Victor and the next few years provided him with greater emotional stability than at any other period of his life.

Trevor Peacher is weak of feature and personality. He is servile in the face of authority yet capable of foul language and violence towards weaker elements. He had been sentenced to seven years' imprisonment for a vicious attack on a young paper boy, imprisoning the victim in his flat and ensuring silence by threats of violence when the boy's parents knocked at the door.

Trevor was particularly attracted to black boys. In conversation he salivated about the colour and softness of their skin; it was inevitable that he would be attracted to Victor when they were thrown together in prison. Attachment developed into a firm relationship and the men set up home together when they were released, jointly purchasing a small flat in Wolverhampton. Trevor now had the chance to indulge his lover, showering him with gifts, including the Sapporo car, which he had customized in line with Victor's specifications.

All appeared to be domestic bliss: while Trevor earned the wages the obsessively tidy Victor cleaned, scrubbed, cooked, washed and ironed. He worked for some time as a van driver for the Crypt Association and it was during this time that he kidnapped the newsboy at Pattingham.

There was only one fly in the ointment of the couple's relationship. In prison Victor had been unaware of Trevor's liking for hard liquor. For some inexplicable reason the young man had a puritanical view of alcohol and tobacco and never indulged in either vice. Disharmony between the two was always caused by Trevor's routine consumption of half a bottle of scotch while watching television, as he enveloped himself in a haze of cigarette smoke.

Peacher was intelligent and hard-working. He was never out of employment and secured a job as a manager at the Mander Paint Company. Eventually he secured a job for his lover at the same establishment.

Detectives given the task of interviewing both men knew instinctively that they were hiding something, and though there was ample evidence to link Miller with Richard Holden, the main object was to find Stuart Gough. Although they dare not say so publicly Cole and Mayo were now convinced he would not be found alive.

Peacher was the first to crack. He was interviewed by Detective Sergeant Viv Howells and Detective Constable Tony 'Barney' Barnes. They made an excellent team. Barney, one of the most experienced detectives in the force, is a wily and tenacious old fox who supplemented the incisive intelligence of his younger supervisor. After twenty-four hours their persistence paid off and Peacher admitted he was telling lies. Distancing himself from any responsibility he confessed that he couldn't provide his lover with an alibi for the weekend of Stuart's disappearance.

For a week he had been in a drunken stupor. On the Monday morning they set off to visit Peacher's elderly mother in Norwich. Along the motorway a furious row broke out about Peacher's drinking, and Victor turned the car round and returned to the flat. Peacher drank himself senseless and was only aware of his partner's presence at intervals during the week when Miller returned to the flat to replenish the whisky bottle. He finally sobered himself up on the Sunday afternoon of Stuart's disappearance.

He heard the dustbin cover being replaced before Victor came into the flat on Sunday evening. He was covered in mud and said, by way of explanation, that the car had got stuck in a gateway. His clothing was put straight into the automatic washer and he spent an hour in the shower. His training shoes had been discarded in the dustbin and were never found.

Peacher's revelations were enough for a change of tactics, and Cole quickly conferred with Eamon Croft, who was interviewing Miller.

Croft returned to the interview room. He had little to say: 'Look, Victor, I know you kidnapped Richard Holden, you know you did it and what's more you know that I know. Why can't you admit it?'

'Because of the wider implications.'

Croft knew what he meant. Miller knew enough about detectives to realize that if he admitted anything they would link all the incidents together and he would find himself answering for Stuart Gough. Although as yet the boy's name had not been mentioned to him he was mystified as to why they had concentrated on Holden. He had not appreciated the tactics employed to secure his continued detention.

There was now enough evidence to charge him with offences committed on Richard Holden and Cole decided to do so without further delay. Immediately afterwards Miller was told he was being further detained for questioning about Stuart Gough. Cole hoped that the first mention of the boy's name would show that he meant business and shake Miller to his roots. The only reaction was a smirk and shrug of the shoulders as he turned back towards the sanctuary of his cell.

While the tactical exercise was played out at Hereford police station the search for the missing boy continued. It had extended to parts of Staffordshire, the West Midlands and mid Wales.

The Pattingham newspaper boy had come forward with his story. Detectives spent days touring Staffordshire and Shropshire until he identified the fields where he had been assaulted. They were at the isolated hamlet of Catstree near the country town of Bridgnorth.

Miller was prepared to talk about his movements during the week he had fallen out with his lover. Essentially it amounted to driving around aimlessly in a fit of depression. He was at pains to distance himself from Herefordshire and claimed he spent most of the time at favourite beauty spots in Rhayader, mid Wales and Kinver Edge, Staffordshire. This prompted large-scale searches in those areas, but it was like looking for the proverbial needle. In truth, it was more of a public relations exercise than an undertaking with any hope of success. It was important for police activity to continue so that press and public attention would be sustained. Continued information from the public was essential in the frantic search for evidence to connect Miller to the abduction.

Meanwhile the interrogation continued. Time was running out for Cole, who knew that Miller would soon be remanded to prison. If he could escape the continuous questioning he would be able more easily to resist the psychological pressure to expose Stuart's whereabouts; there was by now no doubt in the detective's mind that he had killed the boy, but he knew that if he did not find the body he would have insufficient evidence to prove his case.

Late on Friday afternoon it was confirmed that Miller was responsibile for Holden's abduction. A paint sample taken from the gatepost at the entrance to the orchard was matched to paint on the Sapporo.

In another development he was positively connected with the attempted abduction of Antony Dingley – on the evidence of his lover. Trevor Peacher had resisted all efforts to get him to admit more than having provided Victor with the false alibi.

He had been released on bail while further enquiries were made. Once at liberty he hit the bottle. The attendant press corps can always recognize a dummy when they see one and made sure his supply was adequately replenished. It was not long before television cameras were in the flat and viewers were treated to the spectacle of him wallowing in self-pity. A couple of hours later Viv Howells and 'Barney' knocked at his door and felt his collar for a second time. He had made a televised admission that he had perverted the course of justice in supplying an alibi to protect his friend.

Back at Hereford police station Peacher looked up bleary-eyed as David Cole and Allen Mayo entered his cell. He was the first to speak: 'I'm a fucking disaster, ain't I?'

'It's make-your-mind-up time, Trevor my lad' was the reply. 'You know the only thing I'm interested in is finding that boy. Whether you had anything to do with it or not, you know a lot more about this whole business than you've told us yet. Your star performance on telly last night assures you a place in history as the man who told lies to protect Vic Miller – if you want to go on doing that, don't expect much mercy from the public at the end of the day.'

His brief taste of freedom obviously helped put matters into perspective and he blurted out, 'I know nothing about the Gough kid – if I did I'd tell you. I asked him about it often enough. That week he was always watching the news on the telly. He only told me he was the bloke who followed that other kid on the Saturday – I knew it had to be him when I saw that photofit.'

He had now supplied enough evidence for a further charge of the attempted abduction of Antony Dingley to be levelled against his lover, and he knew it. The detectives were treated to another outburst of remorse, but they could not be accused of excessive sympathy.

Miller was utterly oblivious to the feelings of anyone. The Gough family were in despair, but all he was concerned about was his relationship with Peacher. The Holden and Dingley inquiries were in the bag, but Stuart Gough was still missing.

Late on the Friday evening Cole and Mayo were seeking inspiration for the next move together with Detective Inspector Ernie Robinson of the Regional Crime Squad. 'He ain't shown too much conscience yet, Gaffer – but what if we took him round all these places being searched. If he saw all the bloody trouble he is causing it might give him a twinge, or we might just clock some reaction at a particular place which could give us a pointer. We'd take his brief with us so nobody could object.'

The suggestion made sense as a last resort and meticulous plans were made for the route. Miller, probably thankful for a breath of fresh air and relief from the continual questioning, agreed to go.

Psychology forms a major part of the detective's armoury and the three who discussed the Saturday outing were intent on exercising as much pressure as possible to obtain a reaction from the prisoner. The route would begin at the least important locations, to lull him into a false sense of security, and would end at a place he would no doubt recognize. He had no idea that the detectives knew anything about the hamlet of Catstree or the events which had taken place there three years before.

Early on the Saturday morning the party set off. The solicitor sat beside the driver and Miller was wedged in the back seat between Ernie Robinson and his detective sergeant. They headed for mid Wales before returning to Kinver Edge and on to Hagley; round Stuart's route and past his home; along Antony Dingley's path of terror. Not a flicker of recognition or reaction crossed his face, although he was obviously under considerable emotional strain.

Lastly they made their way to Pattingham. Victor hadn't realized the police knew, for they hadn't mentioned it since he had been in custody. Cole had kept it up his sleeve as a little surprise. Then, as they drove from Pattingham towards Catstree Miller became tense. The car eventually stopped at the edge of the field.

'We'll stretch our legs here for a couple of minutes, Vic.'

Ernie got out of the car, followed by Victor, handcuffed to the sergeant.

'This place ring a bell?'

Miller shook his head but his eyes told the wily detective all he needed to know. They had struck a nerve. Miller now knew he faced serious charges against three young boys – God alone knew how long he faced in prison.

Ernie Robinson let him stew in silence on the hour-long journey back to Hereford. As darkness fell the party returned and Miller conferred with his lawyer.

* * *

Having seen little of his family for two weeks David Cole promised them a meal that Saturday evening. He was hopeful of a development, even if not over-optimistic, so had booked an early table at a favourite restaurant in the West Midlands. Having just settled into the first course, his bleeper sounded and the display panel showed the words: 'Phone Incident Room – NOW!!!' Miller and his solicitor, Mr Anthony Davies, wished to see him immediately.

Shortly before nine o'clock the chief superintendent and Allen Mayo entered the interview room.

'Miller, you are still under caution – do you understand? I understand you wish to accept responsibility for the abduction and death of Stuart Gough – is that correct? Will you show me where his body is?'

He received affirmative nods of the head to all three questions.

Soon afterwards a convoy left Hereford and took the Ledbury Road. It was pouring with rain and blowing a gale. For nearly two and a half hours they meandered through country lanes as Miller tried to get his bearings. They crossed and recrossed the Ledbury-to-Gloucester road several times, traversed a swollen ford and got stuck in a narrowing lane. Just before midnight they stopped alongside a wooded gully. The timing was probably a deliberate attempt by Miller to emphasize the macabre.

A small party, guided by the handcuffed prisoner, struggled along a water-filled gully. Three hundred yards from the road they reached a barbed-wire fence and Miller indicated that they should climb over and go a further twenty yards to a holly tree. What they wanted to find was buried under leaves behind the tree. He was rooted to the spot and refused to go further.

A human foot poking from beneath the leaves told Cole the search was over. So remote was the spot that it is unlikely the boy would have been found for years.

Back on the roadway Cole was clearly shaken. In all the experiences they had shared Mayo had never before seen him like this. Ashen-white, with sweat streaming from his brow, Cole had clearly been under strain for the previous few days, and it was beginning to tell. The co-ordination of a huge police inquiry in such emotional circumstances is no easy task. The additional pressures induced by public concern and a stubborn suspect with time on his side are not readily appreciated by anyone who has not been subjected to them. He also knew his personal ordeal was not over for there was the recovery of the boy's body to come and the matter of the autopsy.

'Are you OK, David?'

'I'll be all right – we must tell his family we've found him.'

His first thoughts were for the Goughs. A detective was dispatched to break the dreadful news and offer what comfort he could. In the future the family would be supported by an admirable clergyman and many members of the community, but there was precious little anyone could do to alleviate their grief and suffering at that particular time.

'Herbie' Perriton, the senior scientific officer, approached. 'Shall I make the necessary arrangements, Boss?'

Cole knew what he meant. The scene of any murder is an area of intense, careful activity to discover the smallest particle of evidence. Involving teams of photographers, scientists and a pathologist, the process can take days and it is invariably many hours before the team is assembled and the body removed after preliminary examination. The senior detective always prided himself on his businesslike approach to this task, as it had often paid dividends. This time, however, his professionalism lapsed and he shook his head.

'Uncover the boy carefully, Herb, and take photographs as you go. We know he's dead and who killed him. He's not going to stay out here another night. Take him to Hereford as soon as you can. We'll do the scene in daylight.'

Perriton was clearly taken aback, though he understood the sentiments behind the instruction. Perhaps the old bastard wasn't as hard as he was always cracked up to be.

Having already been warned to stand by, the pathologist patiently sat by the phone, ready to drive off anywhere in the large geographical distribution of West Mercia, which includes Herefordshire, Worcestershire and Shropshire. The body might even be further away – there was some speculation that Miller had gone into Wales at some time. He waited and waited, but the phone never rang. Perhaps they were having more difficulty getting him to talk than they had anticipated? Acland went to bed with one ear cocked for the phone. He slept poorly that night and had rigged the radio to turn itself on to wake him in the morning. The radio news revealed that

Stuart's body had been found in Bromsberrow, near Ledbury, late the previous night. Had he missed the phone call? Had he slept through it? Had the children or the dogs knocked the phone off the hook accidentally? He was cross with himself and embarrassed that he may have let down West Mercia and David Cole. He takes some pride in the ability to be available and respond quickly to calls for his services.

The phone rang. It was West Mercia control room. They asked him to attend Hereford mortuary. He was told that Miller had shown them where the body was to be found the night before, and that David Cole in his 'generosity' had decided that the examination needn't take place there and then, but could wait until the morning. There was nothing to be gained by examining the scene or making the examination in the middle of the night. Acland mumbled that he would have been somewhat grateful if somebody had let him know what was going on a little earlier. He was not at his best that morning. Stuart had gone missing on 17 January, Acland's own birthday – a coincidence that will doubtless add a tinge of sober reflection to the anniversary celebrations.

Acland attended the mortuary at Hereford Hospital at midday on 31 January. He took with him Dr Whitwell, a new consultant colleague, who was becoming interested in forensic matters, and indeed became very experienced very quickly. There is no point in describing the injuries suffered by this poor boy at the hands of his murderer. They add nothing to the story. Miller went as far as his own remaining self-respect would allow him in admitting to most of the injuries. The end, when it came, was mercifully quick for Stuart. The timing of that end was chosen by Miller. Others might want the same choice over his fate.

The distressing story of Stuart Gough is not enhanced by any more detail. Evidence connected Miller's car to the gully and the boy's body. He made a full confession which included attacks on twenty-nine other boys over a number of years. If Stuart Gough had not died his place would inevitably have been taken by some other unfortunate child. Victor Miller had prowled the countryside for a week seeking a victim; several had lucky escapes. His perverted lust had reached a point where it could only be satisfied by death.

When he appeared before magistrates the following Monday Miller instructed his solicitor to make an unprecedented statement. He publicly accepted responsibility for Stuart's death and asked to receive the maximum possible sentence. He said he wanted to avoid causing more distress to Stuart's family.

One or two imponderables remained. Miller drove Stuart over forty miles to his death, removed everything from the boy and drove eighty miles in the opposite direction, past his home town, to the edge of the Staffordshire moors. He selected a suitably marshy area and buried the clothing, newspaper bag, inhaler and knife. Police never found the blindfold which always figured in the attacks, although Miller maintained it was buried in the same place.

Victor Miller always shied away from the unpleasant aspects of his crimes, particularly any suggestion that he stupefied or drugged his victims. He said he relied on fear induced by the knife. The blindfold may have proved otherwise, and it is probably the reason he disposed of it elsewhere and kept the location to himself.

In a gateway near the buried property deep ruts confirmed the story that his vehicle had stuck in the mud. He had, according to his own account, relied upon superhuman strength to lift it free. Was the overweight sadist capable of such a feat of strength or did someone help him?

Everyone in Hagley had been drawn into the tragedy of Stuart's death, and shock and anger were the mixed emotions which greeted the dreadful news when it finally came. The village rallied round the family and such support must have given them some comfort.

Shortly afterwards the parish church was packed for a memorial service. David Cole and his wife slipped quietly into an adjoining annexe filled with grieving residents. As the service was relayed by loudspeaker he found it a poignant moment after the stress of the previous three weeks. At the end he quickly walked away. He had done his best, but the end had been unsatisfactory. Stuart was dead and nothing would bring him back.

On Thursday, 3 November 1988 Miller appeared before Mr Justice Otton at Birmingham Crown Court. Most of the seats were taken by the press and there was room for only a few members of the public; the usual ghouls formed a queue outside the court. The prisoner stood in the dock flanked by prison officers whose eyes never left his face for a second. Just before the judge entered Cole noticed a familiar face on the opposite side of the room – a face pale with hatred and revulsion. It was one of Miller's early victims, now a man, who had come to watch the final act.

It was an anti-climax for the eager reporters, who were not treated to the feast of detail they had hoped for. The case for the Crown was sympathetically and adequately outlined by Anthony Palmer QC. His colleague for the defence, Gareth Williams QC, was equally brief. 'It would be gratuitous indecency,' he said, 'if I made any submission on these facts.'

He could only rely upon the one mitigating factor that Miller spared the bereaved family further uncertainty when he had led police to the boy's body. Any plea he could have made would have been a futile exercise, because his client had already expressed the wish to remain in prison for the rest of his natural life.

Gareth Williams was gracious enough to comment on the police operation. 'The police treated him impeccably. It was an extremely skilful and intelligent police operation.'

Mr Justice Otton chose his words deliberately. 'You are a sadistic sexual psychopath.... You deliberately chose newspaper boys because they were particularly vulnerable ... I can't see the offence other than as a deliberate, premeditated, cold-blooded killing of a person who could not defend himself.... Your motive was to avoid detection and preserve the relationship you had and everything you had built up with your homosexual lover ... You thought the boy held the only tangible clue to your identity, but you were wrong and the discovery of other youths led to your capture.'

There was a smirk on Miller's face as the judge sentenced him to life imprisonment, adding the caveat that, in his case, life would no doubt mean what it said. Turning on his heels with a grin of satisfaction Miller strode towards the cells.

Surely no one will be insane enough to consider releasing him, for he made no secret of the fact that he may kill again if the opportunity arose. Whether he should continue to have the gift of life is another question. Perhaps Geoff Gough's reaction spoke for many others: 'He should be exterminated.'

A local reporter, trying to keep the story alive after the trial, accused the police of responsibility for Stuart's death. He propounded the view that if they had been quicker to publicize the attack on Richard Holden as he rode from work on Friday night, the parents of newspaper delivery boys in Hagley, forty miles away, would have kept their children off the streets on following days. It was a specious argument and hardly worthy of consideration, yet it posed a reasonable proposition: could anything have been done to save Stuart?

The chilling fact is that the death of a male child was inevitable: Miller's gross personality disorder made it a certainty. Several other boys had lucky escapes and if Stuart had not met his awful end another victim would have been found to satiate the psychopath's perverted appetite.

It is a sorry reflection on modern society that the only remedy sophisticated intellects can provide for such individuals is limited periods of incarceration during which perversions fester and ferment making repetition of offences highly likely. While advances are continually made in the positive aspects of medical science there seems little progress in discovering antidotes for the negative side of the human mind. In the widest sense, therefore, Stuart's life could have been spared – if only the society in which he briefly lived had a different set of priorities.

Postscript

Trevor Peacher was later sentenced to three years' imprisonment for providing his lover with the false alibi – an action which frustrated police inquiries for some days.

7 Motorway Misfortune

The Marie Wilkes Case

Cole's bedside telephone rang at ten to seven on Sunday morning.

'Have you been told about this missing girl on the M50, Gaffer?'

He hadn't.

'I won't bother you with details now, but a pregnant girl vanished off the motorway last night while she was making an emergency telephone call. There's blood at the scene and I don't like the look of it. I think it's going to be one for you. Can you come out? I'll pick you up in half an hour.'

Within an hour Cole was standing at the telephone box on the hard shoulder. Detective Chief Inspector Tony Stanley had briefed him on the way down the motorway.

Marie Wilkes's car had broken down a few hundred yards from the telephone and she left her baby son and eleven-year-old sister in the vehicle while she went for help. The police operator who answered the call asked her to hold the line while he tried to contact her father on another telephone. When he returned the girl had gone.

Within minutes, a police car came across Marie's sister struggling along the hard shoulder with the baby in her arms. A search, which went on until dark, failed to find any trace of the young mother.

In the early hours a night-duty detective went to the telephone box; an intensive search would start at day-break and he wanted to make sure that there was no evidence lying around which would later be trampled on by dozens of size 10 Doctor Martens. His caution was justified; beneath the box he found star-shaped droplets of dried blood. They could have come from the girl or, for that matter, any road-accident victim summoning help on the previous few days of dry weather, but he wasn't taking any chances.

It didn't take Cole long to assess the situation. No woman with the enhanced defensive instincts of pregnancy would leave her child unprotected on a motorway, particularly having just been offered help by a friendly operator on the other end of the telephone. In the fresh morning air he shuddered:

'This girl's dead, Tony. Christ knows where she'll be, but we'll make sure she's not on our patch.'

The local police commander had organized a search along the motorway and through surrounding countryside. Police officers with dogs were in evidence on the hard shoulders as the two detectives returned to their headquarters. There were a hundred and one things to think about in getting an investigation under way, but half-way through the journey Cole interrupted his contemplation:

'We should get some idea of what happened at that telephone from the recording equipment in the control room. She couldn't be snatched without some noise being made.'

There was an embarrassed silence. He looked at Stanley who was shaking his head.

'The equipment was knackered last night. All they got was the operator's voice – nothing from the other end.'

Sod's law was at it again. The events of the next thirty-six hours would show it had only just begun.

The emotive nature of Marie's disappearance ensured immediate press and television interest, particularly when Cole arranged for two children to perform a reconstruction of events near the abandoned car. Information came in thick and fast, and it was a considerable task to secure the services of enough detectives to follow all the leads.

At the end of the day the investigators received an assurance that there was no trace of the girl four miles either side of the telephone box. Cole was still not satisfied and asked for the search to be intensified the following day. Marie Wilkes could have been taken anywhere in the country within hours of her abduction, but experience told him the chances were that she was not far away. It is rare for a rapist or killer to travel far with a reluctant victim or dead body. For the time being he placed his hopes on the norm rather than the exception.

'Search everything again, within a mile radius of the telephone. Then extend it half a mile at a time.'

In the event the instructions were unnecessary.

After thirty-six hours without sleep Cole went home for tea on Monday evening intent on a nap before returning for the evening de-briefing. He settled to watch the six o'clock news and the telephone rang.

'She's been found, Gaffer – dead I'm afraid.'

'Where?'

'On the motorway embankment about four miles from the telephone – quite near Junction 1.'

Stanley held the telephone away from his ear, anticipating a reaction. He had drawn the short straw to break the news that there appeared to have been an almighty cock-up in the searching.

There are two bridges near the western approach to Junction 1: the first crosses the River Severn and the second an area of marshland. A witness had seen something of interest near one of the bridges on the evening of Marie's disappearance and two young detectives returned with him to identify the exact spot on Monday tea-time. The unfortunate girl's body lay at the bottom of a steep embankment about fifteen feet from the road and within sight of anyone making even a cursory examination. The police officer who had been allocated the particular stretch of motorway misunderstood his instructions and searched an adjoining area. The bank where the girl lay was the only section which had not been thoroughly examined. Anyone can make a mistake, and there are bloody fools in any organization, but David Cole seemed over-blessed by their presence when it came to finding dead bodies.

Stanley did not relish the prospect of visiting the scene with his volatile boss but found him surprisingly taciturn. The agonizing wait for the inevitable was over and now Cole had something to give him a start in his search for evidence.

'Get Peter Acland and the forensic boys there as soon as you can. We've only got about three hours of good light left and I want to know what that scene can tell us before dark.'

Like most people in the country Acland was well aware of the disappearance of the young housewife. Like most of them, apart from her family, who understandably clung to the possibility of her return, he feared the worst. He saw a news flash that the body of a young woman had been found and within seconds he got the call.

In less than an hour he arrived at the M50 junction – good going for a clapped-out Ford Escort estate, which, as usual, was cluttered with rubbish and severely unwashed. The driver did not look much better. Not noted for sartorial elegance at the best of times, he had just finished a sessions of gardening. Perhaps it was not unexpected that the police sergeant directing all traffic off the M50 should look slightly incredulous as Acland sought to defy his implicit instruction.

'I think actually they may want me at the scene. I'm the Home Office pathologist'.

The officer examined his identification card.

'Sorry, sir, I think we can safely assume they might want you there. I thought you were another bleeding reporter trying it on. Follow that patrol car.'

David Cole emerged from a group of detectives, dressed head to toe in white protective clothing.

'Hello, Pete. This isn't going to be pleasant. Can we make a start as soon as possible?'

The detective and the doctor were in business again.